INTERNATIONAL RELATIONS AND THE FUTURE OF OCEAN SPACE

INTERNATIONAL RELATIONS AND THE FUTURE OF OCEAN SPACE

STUDIES IN INTERNATIONAL AFFAIRS NO. IO

Edited by Robert G. Wirsing

Published for the Institute of International Studies
University of South Carolina
by the

UNIVERSITY OF SOUTH CAROLINA PRESS
COLUMBIA, SOUTH CAROLINA

Library of Congress Cataloging in Publication Data

Symposium on International Relations and the Future
of Ocean Space, University of South Carolina, 1972.
  International relations and the future of ocean space.

  (Studies in international affairs, no. 10)
  Includes bibliographical references.
  1. Maritime law—Addresses, essays, lectures.
2. Marine resources—Law and legislation—Addresses,
essays, lectures. 3. Maritime pollution—Law and
legislation—Addresses, essays, lectures. I. Wirsing,
Robert, ed. II. Title. III. Series: South Carolina.
University. Institute of International Studies.
Studies in international affairs, no. 10.
JX4408.S94 1972   341.44'8   73–14938
ISBN 0–87249–303–2

CONTENTS

Foreword by Richard L. Walker — vii

Acknowledgments — ix

Contributors — xi

Introduction — 3

I SPECIAL DOMESTIC INTERESTS AND UNITED STATES OCEANS POLICY — 10
  H. GARY KNIGHT

II A LAW OF THE SEA CONFERENCE—WHO NEEDS IT? — 44
  ROBERT L. FRIEDHEIM

III NEW APPROACHES TO CONTROL OF OCEAN RESOURCES — 67
  LEWIS M. ALEXANDER

IV A REGIME FOR WORLD OCEAN POLLUTION CONTROL — 83
  E. W. SEABROOK and ALBERT W. KOERS

Appendixes — 117

Index — 143

FOREWORD

Those of us who have been engaged in the educational enterprise over the years have often noted how vocabulary can lend thrust to or condition thinking. All too frequently, economic, strategic, and political thought has been dictated by what Eugene Staley has called "the myth of the continents"—with the usual assumption being that land connects and the seas divide. Thus, through much of the early part of this century our economic and political vocabulary concentrated on concepts embodied by such words as Europe or Asia. It has only really been since World War II that we have come to appreciate adequately the importance and linking role of the oceans. The breakthrough was probably with the creation of the North Atlantic Treaty Organization which put easily traversed ocean space at the center of its concern. Today more than ever before students of international politics are aware of the crucial role of the oceans in the strategic future. In place of concern for delimitation of boundaries on land, we are now grappling with crises over territorial limits on the sea; in place of economic implications of terrestrial resource allocations, we now must define patterns of access to the resources in the oceans; in place of the positioning of armies, we have learned to concern ourselves with the strategy of sea-launched ballistic missiles.

A look into the future of ocean space is overdue. Thus it was that the Institute of International Studies readily agreed to support the initiative of Professor Robert G. Wirsing in organizing in the spring of 1972 the conference which is reflected in this volume. The authors of the chapters have contributed to what we hope is the beginning of some new patterns of thinking in international relations. Professor Wirsing himself has given effort and imagination in pulling together and making a unified volume of the four papers which were discussed at the conference.

I feel that *International Relations and the Future of Ocean Space* as #10 in our Studies in International Affairs series will be a welcome addition to the growing body of literature in the field of international relations.

May 15, 1973   Richard L. Walker
James F. Byrnes Professor of
International Relations

ACKNOWLEDGMENTS

Numerous persons played a role in the preparation of this volume. My special thanks go to the five contributing authors for their exceptional cooperation at all stages of the project. I am grateful as well to all those who participated in the Symposium on International Relations and the Future of Ocean Space, particularly Bruce W. Nelson, Vice Provost for Advanced Studies and Research; W. Hardy Wickwar, Daniel Vaughn, Robert M. Rood, and James G. Holland, Jr., of the Department of Government and International Studies; George D. Haimbaugh, Jr., and Robert L. Felix of the School of Law; Donald M. Chaffee, Department of Economics; William R. Stanley, Department of Geography; F. John Vernberg, Director of the Belle W. Baruch Coastal Research Institute—all of the University of South Carolina; also Charles Pitman, Office of the Legal Advisor, Department of State, Washington, D.C.; Donald C. Bergus, Diplomat-in-Residence, Department of Government and International Studies, University of South Carolina, and formerly Head of the US Diplomatic Mission to the United Arab Republic; Nils Andren, Member of the Swedish Institute of International Affairs, Stockholm, Sweden; and John F. Hussey, Oceanography Counselor, Senate Subcommittee on Oceans and Atmosphere, Washington, D.C.

I am greatly indebted to Vincent Davis, Director of the Patterson School of Diplomacy and International Commerce and Patterson Chair Professor of International Studies, The University of Kentucky, and Captain Gilven Slonim, Vice President, Oceanic Educational Foundation, Falls Church, Virginia, who read the manuscript and made many highly insightful suggestions to improve it.

I want to acknowledge with thanks the kind provision of display materials for use during the Symposium by the National

Oceanographic and Atmospheric Administration, Department of Commerce, Washington, D.C.

Mrs. Cloris A. De Groot unerringly typed the manuscript and made helpful editorial suggestions.

Lastly, I wish to express my deep gratitude to my colleagues of the Department of Government and International Studies, who provided the intellectual stimulus to undertake the project; to D. Bruce Marshall, Research Director of the Institute of International Studies, who aided in getting the book ready for press; and—most especially—to Richard L. Walker, Director of the Institute of International Studies, whose unstinting support and constant encouragement made the entire venture possible.

Robert G. Wirsing
Columbia, South Carolina

CONTRIBUTORS

Lewis M. Alexander is currently Chairman of the Department of Geography, University of Rhode Island, and Executive Director of the Law of the Sea Institute, University of Rhode Island.

Robert L. Friedheim, formerly Associate Professor of Political Science, Purdue University, is currently a staff member of the Center for Naval Analyses, Arlington, Virginia, an affiliate of the University of Rochester.

E. W. Seabrook Hull, journalist, editor, writer, and consultant in coastal and ocean management problems, is presently Editor of *Ocean Science News, Coastal Zone Management* and *World Ecology–2000* in Washington, D.C.

H. Gary Knight is the Campanile Charities Professor of Marine Resources Law, Louisiana State University Law Center; Member, Advisory Committee on the Law of the Sea (United States Government Inter-Agency Law of the Sea Task Force); Program Coordinator, Louisiana State University Sea Grant Law and Sociology Program.

Albert W. Koers is currently Research Associate at the Institute of International Law, University of Utrecht, the Netherlands.

INTERNATIONAL
RELATIONS
AND THE
FUTURE OF OCEAN
SPACE

INTRODUCTION

International Relations and the Future of Ocean Space

Over many centuries, mankind has grown accustomed to conceiving of the environment largely in terms of areas of land space, divided and redivided among innumerable claimants, and inhabited by a motley assortment of culturally distinct societies. Though contentment with the particular boundaries established in any era has rarely been complete, few have questioned the fundamental propriety of drawing them and of enforcing their maintenance. Nothing seems more natural (at least to moderns) than the subdivision of continents into nations, and nations into provinces and subprovinces, with each tier of space authorized more or less exclusive prerogatives in connection with political constitution, social organization, and economic management of resources native to the area. Whether or not we attribute this separatist drive to some primordially ingrained "territorial imperative," to consciousness of racial or cultural differences, or more simply to the lack of political technology equivalent to the task of building more highly integrated systems of community, we are compelled to realize that man has ranged himself across the earth in compartments and devised an immense array of institutions, attitudes and techniques to reinforce the pattern.

Though coastal dwellers have long traveled on, under, and over ocean space, the vast domain of the seas has remained largely exempt from this ancient and potent urge to permanently divide. True, great naval powers in the past have established spheres of influence on the seas; and countless instances of intersocietal violence over the control of sea lanes, lucrative fishing beds, and rights of passage can easily be recalled. But the tradition of freedom of the seas has persisted into the twentieth century with a strength barely less than the tradition of sovereign exclusivity associated with land space.

Today, the traditions of territorial exclusiveness and open seas are coming simultaneously under increasing challenge. It is repeatedly declared that the conventional rules regulating interstate relations are no longer well adapted to the technical capacities of man on land or sea, much less to his need for the management of conflict. Scientific advance is "blurring" the old boundaries, "shrinking" the globe, and confronting every society with the stark necessity for erecting new constitutional frameworks more responsive to the "instantaneous" and "total" reach of technologically revolutionized civilization.

The confusion into which we have been thrown is compounded with respect to ocean space in that here, in what comprises three-fourths of the earth's surface, we are met at once by the revoluton in technology (which may make anachronistic the old freedom) *and* by the absence of a regime rooted in the habits of territorial occupancy that might afford precedents for the effective distribution of ocean authority. Boundaries are not merely blurred; they simply do not exist in any great measure. If, in any new regime, deeply ingrained concepts of the ordering of human communities are to prevail, and the traditional freedom to disappear, then according to what formula are the aspirations of almost 150 nation states containing well over three billion citizens to be accommodated? By what mutually agreeable process is a partitioning to occur? On the other hand, if ocean space is *not* to be carved up into national jurisdictions, how are we to go about erecting the machinery that will realistically provide for international jurisdiction? How are the interests of the self-assertive and numerous developing states to be balanced against the interests of the less numerous but by far more technologically able developed states? The interests of coastal to be harmonized with non-coastal states?

The dilemmas that are rapidly arising from the enormous enlargement of human capacities to use the oceans are not confined to matters of international relations. Particularly among current ocean users, internal interests (coastal and distant water fishermen, the military, the oil and gas industry, to name but a few) are presently girding for battle over national policies whose short- and long-term effects are bound to have differential impact on their various constituencies. How is any government to reconcile its comprehensive national interest vis-a-vis other nations while at the same time reconciling the often competitive interests within its borders? How far should considerations of the global community's interests, say, in environmental policing, in fisheries management, or in the equalization of access to ocean resources, be permitted to override the narrower, but no less imperative, interests of national security, coastal waters fishing, or oil and gas recovery on the continental shelf?

Placed in combination, alternative national and international policy options present a truly formidable array of issues, remarkable not only for their intractability but for the lack of specialized knowledge which pervades most discussions of them. Political, economic, legal, and ecological issues are entwined in a welter of national, regional, and international proposals for reform of the existing regime, while knowledge sufficient to cope with any of them remains at a primitive state.

It was increasing awareness of the need not only for ocean specialists but for the scholarly community in general to grapple with these issues that led the Institute of International Studies to convene a Symposium on International Relations and the Future of Ocean Space at the University of South Carolina on 11–12 April 1972. Scholars representing the disciplines of law, economics, political science, international relations, geography, geology, and marine biology, as well as representatives of the executive and legislative branches of government, and career diplomats, were invited to participate in four sessions concerned with the various dimensions of the oceans policy debates. Papers presented at this symposium formed the basis for the four essays contained in this volume.

Gary Knight's essay surveys the major US interest groups concerned with current oceans policy formulation. Persuaded that some interests—in particular the Department of Defense—have had a lopsided impact on US ocean proposals, Knight argues the need for adequate procedural machinery to assure a fair hearing from all sectors of ocean interests. His examination of the essential needs of seven major interest groups (military, petroleum and natural gas, fisheries, scientific research, hard minerals, transportation, and environmental protection) and the response to them of the 1970–1971 US oceans policy proposals calls into question the claim that these proposals were decided upon in light of the best available knowledge and after a reasoned appraisal of all interests involved.

In the second essay, Robert Friedheim raises the question whether a universal lawmaking agency such as the United Nations is the proper forum in which to resolve oceans issues. Since many of these issues are unavoidably laden with powerful and often antithetic political symbolism, it is questionable, in his opinion, whether another UN Conference on the Law of the Sea can meet the expectations of its proponents. His analysis of the politicized nature of the UN General Assembly—where the objectives of the developing countries frequently comprehend far more than the mere resolution of oceans issues—illuminates the vulnerabilities of any universal assembly in which political considerations are paramount and technical resolutions almost beside the point. His conclusion—that perhaps no one needs such a conference and that its tasks might best be managed in politically less sensitive arenas—is a clear challenge to the wisdom of placing too many fragile oceans issues in the delicate UN basket.

Apart from the difficulties of achieving, at either the national or international level, representation of interests adequate and amenable to the task of developing effective and mutually agreeable oceans policies, the oceans debate entails consideration of the complicated set of problems relating to the creation of an economic regime to govern the allocation of ocean wealth. Lewis Alexander's essay analyzes existing and proposed legal regimes for resource recovery, and points out the problems likely to emerge in the effort to harmonize the economic interests of coastal, landlocked, and shelf-locked countries. In addition to surveying the types of living and non-living resources of the sea, Alexander points to the rapid advance of marine technology which is radically increasing man's capacity to recover these resources, all the while nibbling away in an ad hoc manner at the customary rules governing their exploitation. His essay reiterates Friedheim's point that the creation of a new ocean regime—in this case to govern the creation of zones of economic jurisdiction—will depend in large measure on the willingness of the international community to promote skillful and flexible bargaining, and to arrive at compromises.

In the final essay, Seabrook Hull and Albert Koers consider the development of institutional, legal, and regulatory concepts for controlling global marine pollution. In describing various classes of marine pollutants (heavy metals, chlorinated hydrocarbons, petroleum, radionuclides, and thermal energy), the authors illuminate the delicate nature of the ocean ecosystem and emphasize the disastrous effects unregulated usage of ocean space is likely to have. They argue the need for international definition of the environmental responsibility of states, and spell out the problems involved in setting and enforcing international control criteria. They conclude by outlining the functions and organization of an International Environment Protection Agency, whose task it would be to give direction to the increasingly apparent concern of the international community over the fate of the ocean environment.

The four essays in this volume are a deliberate effort to provide a broad survey of oceans issues and political options, presented within an interdisciplinary framework of national and international politics, law, economics, and ecology. They attempt to provide the background essential to comprehend the immensely complicated and multifaceted controversy into which the global community has been plunged willy-nilly by the rapid deterioration of the old ocean regime. Although some of the authors probe the potential features of a new regime and recommend specific steps towards its implementation, the major thrust in all these essays is toward the clarification of issues. Action to resolve these issues, all would agree, must soon be taken to prevent the chaos and anarchy which some believe are already pervading the oceans. But perhaps in no other sphere of international life is inaction (or inappropriate action) so much the product of simple lack of knowledge.

One last comment seems desirable. Although virtually everyone with some acquaintance with ocean problems shares a deep conviction that these stand among the most dramatic and crucial problems of this century, it would be presumptuous indeed to assume any uniformity among them as to how these problems are best to be resolved. Behind any technical proposal for reform may well lie philosophical convictions no more easily reconciled in ocean space than they are on land. For example, one may dispute Knight's overriding contention that domestic interest groups (apart from the Department of Defense) have not had either procedurally or substantively adequate input into the policy making process. Critics of the pluralist school of American political science have argued persuasively that the national interest, when conceived as the by-product of discrete negotiated settlements between government agencies and counterpart interest groups, may suffer more than it is enriched by their participation. Where does one draw the line between the representation of the well-heeled oil and gas industry, with its easy access to government decision makers, and the representation of more than two hundred million citizens, whose implicit faith in the legislative and executive branches of government clearly does not rest upon the assumption that "what is good for the industry is good for the nation"? In the same way, one may question whether Koers and Hull, in elaborating their scheme for international environment protection housed in a universal institution and based on a system of economic sanctions against wrongdoing polluters, have reflected sufficiently upon the experiences of the League of Nations. The singular lack of success of both the League and the United Nations either in maintaining peace or in imposing sanctions on international aggressors surely introduces a note of skepticism, apparent in Friedheim's essay, about the utility of universalist methods of international problem solving.

The dilemma which these authors had to face is that, in the

real world of international politics, oceans issues cannot be neatly separated from the whole range of issues confronting statesmen in national and international arenas. For better or for worse, oceans problems are inextricably linked to such compelling considerations as national security, alliance strategy, the "energy crisis" of the industrial states, and the "development crisis" of the economically impoverished states. As several of these essays make abundantly clear, the paramount concern of the Third World states is to overcome the widening gap between themselves and the industrialized regions of the globe. The immense discrepancy in levels of development, whatever else it may have in store for the international community, will unavoidably bear upon the fate of ocean space. Pretentious claims on behalf of the priority of oceans problems will not preclude it. It will test the political good sense of all national leaders—and the experts who advise them—to keep the oceans debate from falling into the category either of utopian exhortation or self-serving rhetoric.

The contributors to this volume, while sensing the urgency of oceans problems and the dire need to risk conclusions even in the absence of complete information, have focused their efforts on the monumental and—at this stage—crucial problem of clearly setting forth the issues. Their conclusions may not be acceptable to all, but one may hope that a fuller knowledge of the human stake in the oceans—and the valid grounds for disputing that stake—will contribute at least to a reasoned debate over the future of ocean space.

I

SPECIAL DOMESTIC INTERESTS AND UNITED STATES OCEANS POLICY[1]

H. Gary Knight

On 17 August 1967, Ambassador Arvid Pardo, then representative of the Permanent Mission of Malta to the United Nations, addressed a note verbale to then Secretary General U Thant proposing the inclusion of an item in the agenda of the twenty-second session of the General Assembly entitled "Declaration and Treaty Concerning the Reservation Exclusively for Peaceful Purposes of the Sea-Bed and of the Ocean Floor Underlying the Seas Beyond the Limits of Present National Jurisdiction, and the Use of Their Resources in the Interests of Mankind."[2] In the following five years, significant developments occurred within the United Nations, within national governments, and within private organizations regarding the development of proposed regimes to govern activities in ocean space. Of particular importance to US citizens was the evolution of a national oceans policy. At the time of the introduction of the Maltese agenda item, the United States did not have definite policies with respect to most of the issues involved in the conservation and

[1] The research for this article was supported partially by funds from the Office of Sea Grant Programs (National Oceanic and Atmospheric Administration, Department of Commerce), and partially by funds allocated by Campanile Charities, Inc. for the Campanile Charities Professorship of Marine Resources Law.

[2] United Nations Doc. A/6695, reprinted in *Interim Report on the United Nations and the Issue of Deep Ocean Resources*, 90th Cong., 1st Sess., 1967 (House Report No. 999), p. 7R. See also the statement of Ambassador Arvid Pardo before the First Committee, UN General Assembly, on November 1, 1967, elaborating on his concepts [UN Doc. A/C.1/PV.1515–16], also reprinted in *Interim Report on the United Nations and the Issue of Deep Ocean Resources*, p. 267.

development of ocean resources and the general use of ocean space. Although President Lyndon Johnson had presaged the ultimate US position in his comments at the commissioning of the research ship *Oceanographer* on 13 July 1966,[3] the United States, as well as other technologically developed nations, was taken by surprise as a result of the Maltese initiative. The formal US reaction to the Maltese proposal was given by then UN Ambassador Arthur J. Goldberg on 8 November 1967—a presentation in which US options were carefully protected and a cautious approach was suggested for the obvious reason of gaining time to develop national policy.[4]

As a result, the UN Committee on the Peaceful Uses of the Sea-Bed and the Ocean Floor Beyond the Limits of National Jurisdiction (Seabed Committee hereinafter) was created[5] and was ultimately charged with responsibility to act as preparatory agency for the Third United Nations Conference on the Law of the Sea scheduled for 1973.[6]

[3] The President there stated:
[U]nder no circumstances, we believe, must we ever allow the prospects of rich harvest and mineral wealth to create a new form of colonial competition among the maritime nations. We must be careful to avoid a race to grab and to hold the lands under the high seas. We must ensure that the deep seas and the ocean bottoms are, and remain, the legacy of all human beings. "The President's Remarks at the Commissioning of the New Research Ship, The 'Oceanographer'," 13 July 1966; 2 *Weekly Compilation of Presidential Documents* (No. 28) 930, (18 July 1966) .

[4] Statement of Arthur J. Goldberg before the First Committee, UN General Assembly, on 8 November 1967 (UN Press Release USN–182, 8 November 1967; reprinted in *Interim Report on the United Nations and the Issue of Deep Ocean Resources*, p. 287) .

[5] The Seabed Committee was created by General Assembly Resolution 2467A (XXIII) (1968) [8 *International Legal Materials* 201 (1969)], adopted by 112 votes to none with 7 abstentions. Originally consisting of 42 members, the Committee was expanded to 86 members in December 1970 [General Assembly Resolution 2750C (XXV), operative para. 5] and to 91 members (adding, inter alia, the People's Republic of China) in December 1971 [General Assembly Resolution 2881 (XXVI), operative para. 3]. In December 1970, the Committee was given the task of acting as the preparatory body for the Third United Nations Conference on the Law of the Sea (see note 6 post) .

[6] General Assembly Resolution 2750C (XXV) (1970) called for a Third United Nations Conference on the Law of the Sea to be held sometime dur-

At the July–August 1970, and the July–August 1971, meetings of the Seabed Committee, the US Government submitted draft treaty articles concerning (1) the question of the establishment of a legal-economic regime, and concomitant machinery, to govern the exploration for and exploitation of the non-living resources of the seabed and subsoil beneath the high seas beyond the limits of national jurisdiction, (2) the breadth of the territorial sea, (3) passage through international straits, and (4) preferential fishing rights for coastal states. It is the purpose of this chapter to identify and comment upon the role of special domestic interests in the formulation of this US oceans policy.

Definitions of two terms are necessary. By "special domestic interests" is meant the industries, institutions, or other associational interest groups or lobbies within the United States whose activities involve the use of some portion of ocean space.[7] By "United States oceans policy" is meant only the aforementioned draft treaties submitted by the US Government in 1970

---

ing 1973 unless postponed by the twenty-seventh session of the General Assembly in 1972 on the grounds of insufficient progress of preparatory work. Resolution 2750C identified as potential agenda items for the 1973 Conference: "[T]he regimes of the high seas, the continental shelf, the territorial sea (including the question of its breadth and the question of international straits) and contiguous zone, fishing and conservation of the living resources of the high seas (including the question of preferential rights of coastal States), the preservation of the marine environment (including *inter alia* the prevention of pollution), and scientific research."

[7] "Ocean space" consists of five horizontal strata, as follows (principal present resources or uses of each strata in parentheses): subsoil (petroleum, natural gas, sulphur); seabed (manganese nodules, submarine cables and pipelines, sedentary species of living resources); water column (pelagic fisheries, submarine navigation); surface (navigation); atmosphere (overflight, weather effects through interaction with surface). These physical features are cut by zones of legal jurisdiction affecting different strata—moving seaward from the land, the principal legal zones are: inland waters, the territorial sea, exclusive fisheries zones, other special contiguous zones, the continental shelf, the high seas, and the seabed and subsoil beyond the limits of national jurisdiction. See generally William L. Griffin, "The Emerging Law of Ocean Space," 1 *The International Lawyer* 548 (1967); and H. Gary Knight, "The Draft United Nations Convention on the International Seabed Area: Background, Description and Some Preliminary Thoughts," 8 *San Diego Law Review* 459, 462–477 (1971).

and 1971 to the Seabed Committee, and does not involve other Executive Branch activities, such as subsidies for the maritime industry, or Congressional initiatives, such as the proposed "Deep Seabed Hard Mineral Resources Act."[8]

The role of special interests in the formulation of US oceans policy can be separated into two areas of inquiry—administrative and substantive.[9] In dealing with the subject of foreign policy in general, most attention is given to the substantive outcomes. However, the institutional arrangements for receiving or soliciting the views of special interest groups on substance as well as on strategy and tactics can have a substantial effect upon the outcome of foreign policy. This is particularly true in the current international law of the sea negotiations both because of the broad range of interests involved and the economic magnitude of several of those interests. Accordingly, this chapter also addresses the administrative aspects of the role of special interests in the formulation of US oceans policy. The *method* of taking into consideration the needs of special interests can affect substantive outcomes, and indeed has affected the 1970–1971 US policies in the field of international law of the sea.

Administrative Aspects

There are two basic methods by which special interests can be involved in foreign policy determination. First, individuals can be consulted to review policy proposals which have been reached after appropriate deliberations within the government. In this review panel capacity, individuals representing special interests are urged to comment favorably or critically on the draft policy position. As any lawyer knows, however, it is always an advantage to produce the *first* draft of a contract or other document in negotiations because even though that draft may be modified as negotiations progress, the general approach and

---

[8] "Deep Seabed Hard Mineral Resources Act," S. 2801 and H.R. 13904 (92d Cong., 1st Sess., 1972); see note 43 and accompanying text, post.

[9] On administrative aspects of foreign policy determination in general see Richard A. Johnson, *The Administration of United States Foreign Policy* (Austin: University of Texas Press, 1971).

substantive content of a first draft often give a direction or flavor to a negotiation which can have a decisive effect on the ultimate outcome. Likewise, when the US Government presents to an affected interest group a fait accompli draft policy proposal, critical comments are almost always forced into one of two patterns: (1) objection in toto to the proposed policy, resulting in a complete impasse; or (2) reduction of the role of the special interest group to nit-picking or tinkering with fine points of the draft. Rarely will the government totally reverse a draft policy proposal because of objections on the part of the special interest group, particularly after the government has invested considerable time and effort in the formulation of that policy.

Second, special interest groups can be participants in the policy making process itself. This means involving these individuals at the very earliest stages of policy formulation. It also means giving them access to data—which often is classified at the confidential, secret, and even top secret level—in order that they may intelligently develop, or assist in developing, the policy. Certainly this is a more significant and meaningful role for advisers, and one in which the special interest can have a substantial effect on the outcome. However, for reasons to be discussed below, this approach is relatively untested.

The Department of State has traditionally emphasized the review role for special interest groups. This is not to suggest that particularly strong industry groups were not occasionally able to make sufficiently timely inputs to affect the outcome of draft policy statements. The Department of State, for example, has had institutionalized industrial advisory panels for some time, but such bodies were not extensively utilized, according to most observers, in the policy making stages of the 1970–1971 US oceans proposals.

It should be made clear at this point, however, that the Executive Branch of the government does not develop foreign policy proposals in a vacuum. Obviously, it gathers information on all the affected interests and makes determinations on the basis of national priorities as to how these special interests should be treated in any internationally negotiated agreement. One suspects that the needs perceived by the Department of State for particular interest groups are probably quite closely in line with the needs as perceived by those special interest groups themselves. After all, the interests of special groups are not generally closely held secrets. Nonetheless, there is a significant difference between assuming what the relevant interests are, particularly when it comes to detailed economic analysis, and permitting the special interest group to participate in policy formulation at an early stage.

Criticism of the US Government Inter-Agency Law of the Sea Task Force[10] (Task Force hereinafter) and its predecessors for formulating the 1970–1971 US oceans proposals without adequate use of nongovernmental consultants reached its apex in a paper delivered by Dr. Francis T. Christy, Jr., of Resources for the Future, Inc., at the 1971 Annual Summer Conference of the Law of the Sea Institute in Kingston, Rhode Island.[11] Dr. Christy argued from three premises, (1) "that it is possible to improve decision-making," (2) "that one of the major means for improving the decision-making process is by encouraging and facilitating full, free, and honest discussion of all responsible interests and points of view," and (3) "that successful decisions are ultimately and fundamentally dependent upon the *maximum, public* availability of information."[12] Observing that "information on the government's position and interests in ocean matters is severely and critically restricted," Dr. Christy cited

---

[10] The Task Force is presently chaired by Honorable John R. Stevenson, Legal Adviser to the Department of State, who also heads the US delegation to the UN Seabed Committee, and is composed of representatives of all affected Federal agencies and bureaus, including the Department of State, Department of Defense, Department of Justice, Department of the Interior, Department of Commerce, Department of Transportation, National Security Council, Office of the Vice President, National Science Foundation, Arms Control and Disarmament Agency, Office of Management and Budget, Central Intelligence Agency, US Mission to the UN, and Smithsonian Institution.

[11] See Francis T. Christy, "Research Needs on Ocean Issues: Part One," in Lewis M. Alexander, ed., *The Law of the Sea: A New Geneva Conference,* Proceedings of the 6th Annual Conference of the Law of the Sea Institute (Kingston: University of Rhode Island, 1972), p. 143.

[12] Ibid. Italics in the original.

the Draft United Nations Convention on the International Seabed Area[13] (Draft Convention hereinafter; see summary in Appendix III) and Article III[14] (the US fisheries proposal; see Appendix IV) as examples of US oceans policy proposals which avoided public participation in their formulation.[15] Dr. Christy concluded that there is "significant harm to society when the interested public is not permitted to participate in the formulation of policy," specifying that (1) "secrecy excludes talent and knowledge," (2) secrecy results in "waste of talent . . . available to deal with ocean issues," (3) "secret formulation of policy reduces the choices available to the public and creates an inflexibility in national positions," and (4) since treaties must go through the process of advice and consent, "congressional acceptance is unlikely unless there has been adequate public discussion prior to submission to Congress and unless Congress has been fully informed along the way."[16]

Whether in response to this and other criticism of the administrative aspects of oceans policy formulation, or as a result of efforts initiated earlier, the Department of State announced in February 1972 the formation of the Advisory Committee on the Law of the Sea (ACLOS). The main original function of

[13] United Nations Doc. A/AC.138/25; 9 *International Legal Materials* 1046 (1970). For descriptions and analyses of the Draft Convention see "Draft U.N. Convention on the International Seabed Area: U.S. Working Paper Submitted to U.N. Seabeds Committee," 63 *Department of State Bulletin* 209 (1970), a portion of which is appended to this volume as Appendix III; and H. Gary Knight, "The Draft United Nations Convention on the International Seabed Area: Background, Description and Some Preliminary Thoughts," 8 *San Diego Law Review* 459 (1971).

[14] "Draft Articles on the Breadth of the Territorial Sea, Straits, and Fisheries," United Nations Doc. A/AC.138/SC.II/L.4 (30 July 1971), Article III (see Appendix IV); see also "U.S. Draft Articles on Territorial Sea, Straits, and Fisheries Submitted to U.N. Seabeds Committee," 65 *Department of State Bulletin* 261 (1971).

[15] In fairness, it should be noted that at least one representative of the Government took Dr. Christy to task for his charges concerning development of oceans policy particularly in connection with fisheries negotiations. See the remarks of Burdick H. Brittin, Office of the Special Assistant to the Secretary of State for Fisheries and Wildlife, in Lewis M. Alexander, ed., *The Law of the Sea: A New Geneva Conference*, pp. 146–147.

[16] Christy, note 11 supra, pp. 143–144.

ACLOS was to advise the Chairman of the Task Force and the head of the US delegation to the Seabed Committee.[17] Approximately sixty individuals were appointed to ACLOS, the membership of which was broken down into eight subcommittees: petroleum, hard minerals, international finance and taxation, international law and relations, marine environment, fisheries, marine science, and maritime industries. One member each from the petroleum, hard minerals, marine science, and international law and relations subcommittees, and two members from the fisheries subcommittee (a total of six persons) were given official status as members of the US delegation to the Seabed Committee meeting of March 1972.

The precise role of ACLOS was not spelled out at the time of its creation—certainly the law of the sea proposals already submitted by the United States in 1970 and 1971 precluded its use in the policy making activities relating to the subject matter of those proposals, except in terms of modifications (the review capacity). However, there are many substantive areas not covered by existing US proposals (e.g., scientific research, nonextractive uses of the seabed, and—some would say in spite of Article III—fisheries) and significant questions of strategy and tactics which, it is hoped, will provide ACLOS a policy shaping rather than a review role. The question of the autonomy of ACLOS and its subcommittees was also left unresolved, although one suspects that the subcommittees will take an active role in formulating their own proposals as well as in responding to requests for evaluations by the Task Force.

One obvious problem in connection with the role of ACLOS is that members not assigned to the US delegation to the Seabed Committee were afforded security clearances only to the confidential level and were not permitted to sit in on delegation meetings. This means that such fundamental data as the formal

---

[17] I am a member of ACLOS, assigned to its Subcommittee on International Law and Relations. Any comments about ACLOS in this article are derived from my personal experience with it, and do not divulge any classified or otherwise restricted information concerning ACLOS or the subject matter considered by it.

negotiating instructions from the National Security Council, which are classified as secret, were not available to members of ACLOS. Further, many factual details, particularly concerning the interest and role of the Department of Defense (DOD) in the law of the sea negotiations, were not made available to ACLOS members.[18] A legitimate question then arises concerning just how significant a role in policy formulation ACLOS members can play if access to secret and top secret information is denied to them.

In spite of this criticism, it seems that a substantial advance in terms of opening the administrative system of oceans policy formulation to special interests was made by the creation of ACLOS. What substantive effect this initiative will have remains to be seen.

As already noted, it is apparent that those Task Force members who drafted the four part 1970–1971 US oceans proposals were aware of the essential needs of the major domestic interests in the law of the sea.[19] As also noted, however, this is not the

[18] See for example the author's comments on defense interests in the oceans in H. Gary Knight, "The 1971 United States Proposals on the Breadth of the Territorial Sea and Passage Through International Straits," forthcoming in a special issue of the *Oregon Law Review* on ocean resources law. The lack of explanation from the Department of Defense concerning the necessity for submerged passage through international straits by Polaris/Poseidon class submarines makes evaluation of the US proposal on straits passage extremely difficult.

[19] This paper is, as evidenced by its title, limited to consideration of special *domestic* interests. Nonetheless, it needs to be noted that the drafters of US oceans policy proposals to date have, at least in the Draft Convention, admirably taken a long range foreign policy viewpoint by considering the needs and abilities of other members of the international community in arriving at specific proposals. The term "admirable" is used because it is always tempting (and usually much easier and safer) to produce foreign policy proposals which seem, in the short run, to benefit only our own national economic interests. Accordingly, it should not be thought that criticisms voiced here of current US oceans policy decisions in terms of the role of special domestic interests indicates in any way that such interests ought to be afforded a position of primacy in the total list of factors to be considered. To the contrary, no single special economic interest should be permitted to override decisions that are, in the long run, beneficial to the entire national interest.

same thing as permitting those interests to assist in the shaping of policy. Thus, if there are distinctions between what special interests perceive as their needs from the law of the sea negotiations, on the one hand, and the elements contained in the four part 1970–1971 US oceans proposals, on the other hand, it can be argued that such distinctions stem in part from the fact that such special interest groups were not permitted to enter the policy making process at a sufficiently early stage.

Three further comments need to be made before analyzing the specific interest group situations. First, it is clear that there may be valid justifications for governmental secrecy for reasons of (1) protecting critical military information or (2) preserving a negotiating position. However, and consistent with the criticisms voiced by Dr. Christy, it seems imperative that at least a limited number of knowledgeable representatives of special interest groups must be trusted if the evils of totally secret government decision making are to be avoided.

Second, the status of the DOD as the representative of military interests in the ocean presents a difficult problem since all of the other special interest groups are nongovernmental (though most are, to a greater or lesser degree, subsidized by Federal funds). There may be inquiry as to why the interests of the military establishment are included in the special interest category, yet not other governmental long range interests such as international economic development, international political stability, development of needed energy and food resources, and the like, which might be said to come under the purview of the Department of Commerce, the Department of the Interior, and the Department of State. These and other departments of government clearly represent important ocean interests, and would have to be considered in a more comprehensive analysis. The inclusion of the DOD in this preliminary investigation is a fundamental necessity, however, since it has, along with the nongovernmental special interests identified below, a particularly unique relation with the ocean environment.

A corollary question is whether the DOD ought to be required to participate in policy formulation on the same level as the other special interests, or whether since it is part of the Executive Branch of government itself, it should be entitled to a favored position based both upon the quantitative importance of national security and the fact that it is charged with both the execution and formulation of policy. One problem faced is the difficulty of quantifying the interests of the DOD in the law of the sea. If, for example, one should want to use relatively short term economic product as the measure of the relative importance of two competing interest groups as a method for determining priorities, industries such as the maritime transportation and petroleum groups would greatly overshadow the scientific research and hard minerals interests. But how does one place a value on national security? And how does one consider future value? In the past, the tendency has been to allow the secrecy-shrouded mystique of the Pentagon to largely direct law of the sea policy. Without in any way suggesting that essential national security measures be compromised, it may be argued that the role of special interests in the formulation of US oceans policy would be more productive if all of the participants, at least administratively, had equal access to information and equal access to the policy makers in early stages of policy formulation. This does not mean that accommodations based on some form of quantification of interests might not be made as the substance of the policy was hammered out.

Third, and finally, one must always remain aware that in private as well as public forums, arguments among competing interests are not always resolved on the basis of explicit evaluative criteria, but rather on the basis of effective advocacy. Effective advocacy depends upon a number of factors, principally individual ability, governmental influence, and financial support. A related consideration is the constituency *supporting* particular interests. For example, the petroleum and natural gas industry has been blessed with extremely capable advocates, well financed lobbying efforts, *and* strong support from a large domestic constituency. In contrast, advocates of the interest of freedom of scientific research, although able and articulate men, have suffered from lack of financial support and, even more, from the lack of a national constituency favorable to their interests.

In conclusion, it should be admitted that there are many conflicting interests involved in policy formulation, and that accommodations among them are inherently difficult to make. Even if the perceived needs of all major interest groups could be specifically identified and agreed upon, it would probably be impossible to draft an oceans policy which would fully satisfy each such interest. Nonetheless, some discrepancies could undoubtedly be rectified were changes made in the procedures of policy determination.

Substantive Aspects

The remainder of this chapter will (1) outline briefly the essential needs of the major special interests in the law of the sea, and (2) report how the 1970–1971 US oceans policy proposals responded to those needs. Further, it will offer some critical comments on the gaps (or the absence of gaps) between perceived needs and US oceans policy. The seven special interest groups to which attention is given are military, petroleum and natural gas, fisheries, scientific research, hard minerals, transportation, and environmental protection. The order of treatment should not be taken as indicative of relative importance, either in the author's mind or absolutely.

A. *Military*

The curtain of secrecy surrounding present and future military activities in the ocean makes any evaluation of the perceived needs of the DOD an educated guessing game at best. However, there have been in the last three or four years a few quite excellent analyses of the role of the Navy in the national security system and the essential elements, if not all of the minute details, of the current DOD interests in the law of the sea are reasonably well known.[20] These needs fall into three basic categories:

(1) *The Polaris/Poseidon Nuclear Strike Force.* The Polaris/Poseidon system has become the linchpin of our second strike nuclear capability which is in turn the linchpin of our current nuclear deterrent philosophy.[21] The object is to render undetectable, and therefore indestructible, the submerged Polaris/Poseidon fleet. In order to maximize undetectability the Polaris/Poseidon fleet requires maximum possible submerged mobility. This in turn dictates the narrowest possible belt of maritime territorial sovereignty. It is clear, however, that the worldwide trend is away from the traditional three mile territorial sea and toward a twelve mile territorial sea, or more.[22] As an inhibiting factor on *general* mobility, the expansion from three to twelve

[20] Probably the best study, and one which has been particularly useful in preparing this portion of the paper, is John A. Knauss, "Factors Influencing a U.S. Position in a Future Law of the Sea Conference," Law of the Sea Institute Occasional Paper No. 10 (April, 1971), pp. 2–8 (hereinafter cited as Knauss, "Factors"). See also John A. Knauss, "The Military Role in the Ocean and Its Relation to the Law of the Sea," in Lewis M. Alexander, ed., *The Law of the Sea: A New Geneva Conference,* p. 77 (taken from the above cited Occasional Paper); Leigh S. Ratiner, "National Security Interests in Ocean Space," 3 *Natural Resources Lawyer* 582 (1971); and Leigh S. Ratiner, "United States Oceans Policy: An Analysis," 2 *Journal of Maritime Law & Commerce* 225 (1971). A debt is owed in this and subsequent sections to Dr. Ann L. Hollick of the School of Advanced International Studies (Johns Hopkins University, Washington, D.C.) for permission to review her as yet unpublished doctoral thesis concerning the development of US oceans policy.

[21] Robert A. Frosch, "Military Uses of the Ocean," in *Papers Presented at the Second Conference on Law, Organization and Security in the Use of the Ocean* (1967) 154, 157, 169; and John A. Knauss, "Factors," note 20 supra, pp. 2–3.

[22] The latest Department of State tabulation ["International Boundary Study—Series A—Limits in the Seas—National Claims to Maritime Jurisdictions," No. 36 (January 3, 1972), revised March 31, 1972] shows (for 117 jurisdictions for which data is available) 34 states (29%) claiming 3 or 4 miles, 67 claiming 6 to 12 miles (57.2%; 55 claim exactly 12 miles) and 16 (13.6%) claiming in excess of 12 miles. (See Appendix II for a complete tabulation of national claims.) By comparison, an absolute majority of coastal states still claimed three miles prior to 1958; see Bernard G. Heinzen, "The Three-Mile Limit: Preserving the Freedom of the Seas," 11 *Stanford Law Review* 597, 641 et seq. (1959).

miles is relatively insignificant. The importance of such expansion is that a substantial number of international straits which are now possessed of areas of high seas by virtue of a three mile limit would become territorial waters if the breadth of the territorial sea were expanded to twelve miles.[23] Under the provisions of the Convention on the Territorial Sea and the Contiguous Zone (Territorial Sea Convention hereinafter) [24] submarines are required to navigate on the surface and show their flag when transiting territorial waters.[25] This means that whereas Polaris/ Poseidon submarines may now legally pass through straits such as Gibraltar in a submerged state, expansion of the territorial sea to twelve miles would, without other change in the existing law of passage, require them to surface and show their flag. Accordingly, the DOD sees the necessity for implementing a system of free transit through international straits, including the right of overflight and submerged passage, without control or conditions imposed by the coastal state.

(2) *Intelligence Operations and Traditional Naval Maneuvers.* Obviously, operators of intelligence gathering vessels would prefer the narrowest possible territorial sea, for there is a marked increase in the resolution of electronically and visually gathered data as one moves closer to the source being investigated (of course, narrow territorial sea limits also make one's own shore based security installations more vulnerable to hostile surveillance). Further, traditional uses of naval power, including "gunboat diplomacy," also dictate the narrowest possible territorial sea. Finally, any restrictions which might be placed on warships under a subjective interpretation by the coastal state of the standard of innocent passage under present international law (which would be applicable to an increased number of straits

---

[23] See Geoffrey E. Carlisle, "Three-Mile Limit: Obsolete Concept?" 93 *U. S. Naval Institute Proceedings* (No. 2) 24 (1967). An often quoted figure for the number of straits which would become territorial waters by virtue of expansion of the breadth of the territorial sea from 3 to 12 miles is 116.

[24] Convention on the Territorial Sea and the Contiguous Zone [*done* 29 April 1958, 15 U.S.T. 1606 (1964), T.I.A.S. No. 5639, 516 U.N.T.S. 205, in force 10 September 1964]. The United States is a party to the Convention.

[25] Ibid., Art. 14 (6).

if the territorial sea were expanded from three to twelve miles)
might hamper traditional naval mobility. Thus, on the basis
of these interests as well as the Polaris/Poseidon situation, the
military establishment is interested in a relatively narrow territorial sea and a system of free transit through international
straits.

(3) *Antisubmarine Warfare Tracking and Detection Devices.*
A concomitant of the Polaris/Poseidon fleet's operation is the
necessity for tracking and detecting counterparts from the Soviet
Union or other potentially hostile nations.[26] The desired objective here, of course, is that the seabed and subsoil beyond a
reasonably narrow continental shelf zone be open for the im-
plantation of antisubmarine warfare (ASW) tracking and detection devices. Although not ruling out the need for coastal
state or international community jurisdiction over the exploitation of the resources of the seabed and the subsoil, the regime
desired by the DOD would leave open to use by all states
"other" seabed activities, including the right to deploy ASW
tracking and detection devices.

Examining now the 1970–1971 US law of the sea proposals,
it is interesting to note that *all* of the needs of the military establishment have been met to the fullest possible degree. This
is perhaps another way of saying that the special interest group
known as the Department of Defense has been eminently successful in its attempts to affect the formulation of US oceans
policy. Perhaps we can attribute this to the fact, alluded to
above, that the DOD, unlike other special interest groups, is
itself a part of the government and an integral part of the foreign policy decision making process. We could also attribute it
to the relative importance of national security. In fact, of
course, the DOD was instrumental in raising the oceans policy
question to the level of the White House, which ultimately led
to a Presidential statement on the issue. Without the Department's initiative in this manner, some have suggested, the nation

---

[26] On antisubmarine warfare tracking and detection devices generally, see
Stockholm International Peace Research Institute, *SIPRI Yearbook of World
Armaments and Disarmament* 1969/70 (1970) 106–112, 148–152.

still might be without a Presidential decision on oceans policy. The symbiotic relationship of the Departments of State and Defense with respect to oceans policy is a fascinating study in itself—the Department of State seeks to further certain foreign policy objectives requiring an essentially international seabed regime; the Department of Defense wishes access to the seabed for its ASW devices, narrow territorial seas, and free transit through straits, for which it is willing to trade acquiescence in an international regime (and, for the ASW needs, use its substance). Thus an unusual alliance of the two departments presents a formidable obstacle to interests with other views, e.g., the petroleum industry.

How are the military interests met? The requirements of a relatively narrow territorial sea and free transit through straits were met through the proposed Articles I and II submitted by the US delegation to the Seabed Committee at its July–August 1971 meeting (see Appendix IV). Articles I and II provide in essence for a twelve mile territorial sea and a system of free transit through international straits constituting "the same freedom of navigation and overflight, for the purpose of transit through and over [international] straits, as [is permitted] on the high seas." Needless to say, the content of these two draft articles was dictated by the DOD.

Further, the fear of the military that extensive unilateral claims of territorial sea jurisdiction (to two hundred miles, or more) would seriously inhibit naval mobility was placated by effective internationalization of the seabed beyond the two hundred meter isobath, a process in which coastal state renunciation of rights in that area, coupled with a granting back of resource exploitation jurisdiction *only,* takes out of the hands of coastal states the power to further encroach upon ocean space.

Turning to the military interests in maintaining freedom to implant ASW tracking and detection devices on the seabed, one finds satisfaction of this need in the Draft Convention. That proposal would limit the exercise of *exclusive* coastal state jurisdiction for other than mineral exploitation purposes to the twelve mile limit, since under both the Convention on the

Continental Shelf[27] (which presumably would remain applicable to the two hundred meter isobath) and the Draft Convention (including the Trusteeship Area) ,[28] exclusivity is permitted only with respect to the exploitation of seabed resources and would not, therefore, act as a bar to other uses. The basis for this interpretation is Article 3 of the Draft Convention which provides that the "International Seabed Area shall be open to use by all States, without discrimination, except as otherwise provided in this Convention." The Draft Convention provides "otherwise" only with respect to exploration and exploitation of certain natural resources, presumably leaving all other uses to be covered by the "open to use by all States" proviso of Article 3. As John R. Stevenson noted in introducing the Draft Convention in August 1970: "The rights of states to conduct activities other than exploration and exploitation of natural resources in the International Trusteeship Area and beyond would be expressly protected by the Convention and the International Seabed Resource Authority would be empowered to adopt the additional rules necessary to protect these other uses of the marine environment."[29]

[27] Convention on the Continental Shelf [*done* April 29, 1958, 15 U.S.T. 471 (1964), T.I.A.S. No. 5578, 499 U.N.T.S. 311, in force June 10, 1964]. The United States is a party to the Convention which accords coastal states exclusive sovereign rights for the purpose of exploring and exploiting the natural resources of the continental shelf [Art. 2 (1)] in the area "adjacent to the coast but outside the area of the territorial sea, to a depth of 200 meters or, beyond that limit, to where the depth of the superjacent waters admits of the exploitation of the natural resources of the said areas" [Art. 1].

[28] The Draft Convention expressly and impliedly envisions four jurisdictional zones for the seabed, beginning at the low water mark: (1) a twelve mile territorial sea, in which the coastal state has complete authority, (2) the area out to the two hundred meter isobath, which, outside the twelve mile limit, would be subject to the regime of the continental shelf, (3) the Trusteeship Area, extending from the two hundred meter isobath (or twelve mile limit, if the latter is farther seaward) to the edge of the continental margin, in which the coastal state would have primary administrative rights governing extraction of natural resources, and (4) the International Seabed Area seaward of the Trusteeship Area, which would be purely international in character.

[29] "Draft U.N. Convention on the International Seabed Area: U.S. Working Paper Submitted to U.N. Seabeds Committee," 63 *Department of State*

One can, then, only conclude that as a special interest, the Department of Defense has fared exceptionally well in affecting the outcome of US oceans policy.

B. *Petroleum and Natural Gas*

Like any commercial enterprise, the petroleum and natural gas industries (sometimes referred to hereinafter collectively as the oil industry) are concerned almost exclusively with profit maximization. This can be secured with respect to oil deposits beneath the oceans, the oil industry asserts, only by sufficient security of investment to assure (1) a reasonable rate of return on invested capital and (2) adequate long term protection for that invested capital.[30] Stating its position principally through the National Petroleum Council, the oil industry perceives the extension of coastal state jurisdiction on a worldwide basis over the resources of the seabed and subsoil as necessary for the attainment of these objectives. Since petroleum and natural gas resources are likely to be found in the subsoil of the entire continental structure, but are unlikely to be found beyond that area, the oil industry argues that national jurisdiction should

---

Bulletin 209, 210 (1970) (see Appendix III). Presumably, the Council of the International Seabed Resource Authority could prohibit the implanting of ASW tracking and detection devices, but it is likely that the United States and the Soviet Union would have enough power under the proposed Council structure to prevent any such action, on threat (if necessary) of nonsupport for the seabed regime. In any event, and so long as the nuclear armed submarine is the essential deterrent to nuclear war (which seems to be assured for the foreseeable future by the Strategic Arms Limitation Agreement signed in Moscow as this manuscript was being transmitted for publication), ASW tracking and detection devices will be an integral part of the second strike capability system, and the third world will be as powerless to affect their deployment as it is to outlaw the submarine forces themselves.

[30] On the oil industry's position with respect to oceans policy in general and the Draft Convention in particular, see National Petroleum Council, "Petroleum Resources Under the Ocean Floor: Supplemental Report" (March 1971); "The Proposed Seabeds Treaty: Report of the Marine Resources Committee of the Section of Natural Resources Law of the American Bar Association," 5 *Natural Resources Lawyer* 132 (1972); Luke W. Finlay, "The Draft United Nations Convention on the International Seabed Area—American Petroleum Institute Position," 4 *Natural Resources Lawyer* 73 (1971).

extend to the edge of the continental margin, a boundary roughly approximated by the twenty-five hundred meter isobath.[31] Although couched in much rhetoric about the "energy crisis" and "national needs," the position clearly serves first and foremost the financial interests of the oil industry and it is that need (not real or imaginary national interests) which a seabed regime must satisfy in order to please the industry.

Although the basis for the insistence upon extension of national jurisdiction as the only method for providing sufficient security of investment has never been satisfactorily articulated by representatives of the oil industry, it seems clear that its primary motivation is the maintenance of the status quo regarding negotiating relations between the petroleum companies operating in the oceans and the coastal states. If a narrower continental shelf or seabed boundary were adopted, then the international organization established to regulate activities beyond the limits of national jurisdiction would play a more immediate role in the exploitation of petroleum resources, a role the petroleum companies, for unexplained reasons, do not seem to desire.

How did the oil industry fare at the hands of government policy makers? The Draft Convention would require a renunciation of national interests in seabed resources beyond the two hundred meter isobath and the regulation thereof by an international agency.[32] However, the coastal state receives back in the

---

[31] In fact, the argument has been advanced that the United States *presently* possesses rights to the natural resources of the seabed and subsoil out to the edge of the continental margin, though there is little support for such a position outside the oil industry and its spokesmen:

[T]he wording of the Geneva Convention on the Continental Shelf, the history of its interpretation by the United States at the time of ratification, prevailing current legal opinion, the practice of the United States and other coastal states, and geological and geographical considerations, all combine to make it clear that the legal, natural, and appropriate limits of U.S. sovereign rights over the natural resources of the sea bottom extend out to the edge of the submerged continent, irrespective of depth of water or distance from shore. National Petroleum Council, "Petroleum Resources Under the Ocean Floor" (March 1969), 69–70.

[32] Draft Convention, Art. 1 (2), Art. 2.

Draft Convention certain special rights in an area called the International Trusteeship Area (extending from the two hundred meter isobath to the edge of the continental margin), which give it exclusive powers to determine if, when, where, how, what and by whom the seabed resources are to be exploited,[33] subject only to a few basic guidelines to be enforced by the international agency. It is this residuum of international authority to which the petroleum industry strongly objects. In short, they argue that the treaty should apply the inverse situation, thus allowing the coastal state to have exclusive jurisdiction over seabed resources to the edge of the continental margin, retaining all residual rights, while granting a share of the revenues from that area to the international community.

The failure of the petroleum industry to achieve this last added measure of security of investment certainly cannot be attributed to a lack of input from a reasonably early stage. The petroleum lobby is well financed and well organized, and made its influence felt (in spite of the lack of institutionalized arrangements for so doing) at the highest levels of government throughout the formulation of US oceans policy. One can only surmise that the interest of the Department of Defense in seeking to avoid extension of national sovereignty over areas of high seas (the "creeping jurisdiction" argument)[34] and its desire to restrict as much as possible coastal state jurisdiction with respect

[33] Draft Convention, Appendix C:
Sec. 2.1. The Trustee Party, pursuant to Chapter III, shall have the exclusive right, in its discretion, to approve or disapprove applications for exploration and exploitation licenses.
Sec. 3.1. The Trustee Party may use any system for issuing and allocating exploration and exploitation licenses.

[34] "Creeping jurisdiction" is the name given to the supposed phenomenon that national jurisdiction in the oceans for limited purposes tends to ripen into territorial sea jurisdiction. As a juridical concept, there is little or no basis for the doctrine. As a matter of functional response to a perceived need, coastal states do tend to take whatever jurisdiction is necessary to secure or protect vital national interests. However, there has been no conclusive showing of a relationship between assertion of one form of jurisdiction and an increased probability of that assertion leading to further claims. To the contrary, evidence suggests that each subsequent assertion is independent of earlier moves.

to the seabed in order to maintain its freedom to implant ASW tracking and detection devices, outweighed the arguments of the oil industry for total and absolute security of investment.

The petroleum industry can operate quite securely under the regime envisioned in the Draft Convention. Permitting a residuum of international authority in no way prejudices or threatens to impose unreasonable costs on its operations out to the edge of the continental margin. Thus, it would appear that the other major interest group also fared quite well in the US 1970–1971 proposals.

C. *Fisheries*

The fishing industry's interest in the ocean is bifurcated between the coastal fishermen and the distant water fishermen. Both have a mutual interest in rational management of ocean resources without which living resources might no longer be available for exploitation; but when the issue of allocation of resources arises, the two segments of the industry split markedly. Coastal fishermen, who are not now competitive with technologically advanced foreign fishing fleets and who may be damaged economically by the latter's refusal to abide by standards of good fisheries management, favor expanded US jurisdiction in the ocean in the form of an exclusive fisheries zone to a substantial distance from shore. The two hundred mile limit is often suggested. The coastal fishing industry had some success with this concept in 1966 when it prevailed upon the Congress to enact the twelve mile Exclusive Fisheries Zone Act.[35]

On the other hand, the distant water fishermen, most of whom belong to the tuna industry, favor reasonably narrow limits so as not to prejudice their activities off the coasts of other states. The shrimping industry has a dual interest since it operates both in US coastal waters and off the coasts of Brazil and Mexico, among

---

[35] Exclusive Fisheries Zone Act, 16 U.S.C.A. §§ 1091–1094 (1966) (originally enacted as Act of October 14, 1966, 80 Stat. 908). The Act established a fisheries zone contiguous to the territorial sea of the United States in which this nation exercises "the same exclusive rights in respect to fisheries . . . as it has in its territorial sea."

other states.[36] Finally, those fishermen who exploit anadromous species such as salmon support the principle by which a state's investment in protection of anadromous species while in fresh water is to be rewarded by the exclusion or limitation of participation by other states in the extractive phase of the fishery on the high seas.

How did the fishing industry fare at the hands of the US Government? The US proposal on fisheries is contained in Article III (Appendix IV). The major problem with Article III is that it does not come to grips with the crucial question concerning the relationship between coastal and distant water fishing states. It does provide for a preference for the coastal state in terms of the allowable catch of a stock in areas adjacent to its coast, but also specifies that the percentage of the allowable catch of a stock traditionally taken by the fishermen of other (distant water) states shall not be allocated to the coastal state. In a footnote, it is stated that it is the "view of the United States government that an appropriate text with respect to traditional fishing should be negotiated between coastal and distant water fishing states." This hardly helps resolve the dispute. In part this is due not to the lack of communication between fishing interests and the government (which is alleged in the past to have been substantial)[37] but to the fact that the affected Federal departments (Defense, State, Interior, and Commerce, primarily) have been unable to agree from an internal government policy standpoint on an acceptable resolution of the issue, a situation compounded by changing international perspectives on

[36] The shrimp industry seems to be having the best of both worlds at present. The United States entered into an agreement with Brazil on 9 May 1972, permitting continued US shrimping off Brazil's coast in spite of Brazil's claim of a two hundred mile territorial sea (see "United States and Brazil Sign Shrimping Agreement," Department of State Press Release No. 111, 9 May 1972). If the United States adopted a two hundred mile exclusive fisheries zone (either through unilateral action or by international agreement) the industry could protect its monopoly off its own coast without seriously endangering its rights under the US-Brazilian treaty since nationals of the latter state do not fish off the coasts of the United States.

[37] See note 15 supra.

the subject. Thus, they have really had no meaningful proposal to submit even for review by fisheries interests.

Judging from statements made by US representatives in the March 1972 meeting of the Seabed Committee, however, it seems that the United States is leaning heavily in the direction of supporting expanded coastal jurisdiction over fisheries. Ambassador Donald L. McKernan, in a speech delivered on 29 March, said, inter alia:

> Within the framework of the species approach, and in respect to two types of fish stocks, coastal and anadromous, *we are prepared to consider a greater role for coastal* States. . . .
>
> [W]e are ready to consider whether responsibility for conservation and management of coastal and anadromous species could rest *primarily with the coastal State,* subject to agreed international standards and reviews. . . .
>
> Specifically, we are prepared to consider *whether clear regulatory authority could be vested in the coastal State* with respect to coastal species adjacent to the state's coast and anadromous species throughout their migratory range on the high seas. . . .
>
> Effective management and conservation . . . may be provided *by granting coastal States clear and effective control over all such species,* in the context of protecting other uses of the high seas.[38]

If in fact US policy with respect to fisheries has not crystallized, then the fisheries industry actually stands a reasonable chance of assisting in the formulation of policy. Certainly this is a highly desirable situation, but it is complicated, as mentioned above, by the diversity of interests within the fishing industry itself. This is perhaps best illustrated by the fact that the Fisheries Subcommittee of ACLOS was the only such sub-

---

[38] Statement of Donald L. McKernan, Alternate Representative of the United States to the UN Seabed Committee, Subcommittee II, 29 March 1972 (paraphrased in Summary Records of Subcommittee II, UN Doc. A/AC.138/SC.II/SR.31 at 12–18). Emphasis added.

committee allocated two members to the delegation of the United States to the Seabed Committee—one representing coastal fisheries interests, the other representing distant water interests.

Fisheries, then, did not seem to get the early attention that the military and petroleum interest groups did, at least in terms of favorable results. Yet the position of the fishing industry has not been prejudiced beyond recall; if it can secure internal accord on a proposed international fisheries regime (as recent developments indicate it is doing), the mechanism is present for transmitting that view effectively to the Task Force and, possibly, into US fisheries policy.

D. *Scientific Research*

The position of ocean scientists is clear. They wish maximum freedom of access to all possible strata and areas of ocean space for purposes of conducting research.[39] Falling into essentially three categories—military, commercial, and pure—scientific research has a variety of methods of operation and ultimate applications. The scientific research community, based primarily in universities and private institutions, seeks only freedom for pure research, leaving industry and the Department of Defense to negotiate their own respective needs concerning the other two categories of research. The thorny problem is what constitutes "pure" research, since all data obtained may ultimately have commercial or military value. This paper will not examine the various substantive proposals and arguments on this issue, but they are available for the interested reader in the articles cited in footnote 39.

Many developing countries have expressed an antipathy to-

[39] For background and discussion of the position of the scientific research community, and the issues involved, see William T. Burke, "Marine Science Research and International Law," Law of the Sea Institute Occasional Paper No. 8 (1970) ; John A. Knauss, "Factors," note 19 supra, 18–20; Milner B. Schaefer, "Freedom of Scientific Research and Exploration in the Sea," 4 *Stanford Journal of International Studies* 46 (1969) ; and Thomas A. Clingan, "Scientific Inquiry in the Oceans: Legal Regulation and Responsibility," 6 *Lex et Scientia* 77 (1969) .

ward scientific research, confounding those who view acquisition of knowledge as inherently good, on the bases that (1) it may prejudice their position in negotiations over the disposition of resources on their continental shelves, (2) it may permit the conduct of military activities near their coasts which could impair their national security, and (3) since research almost always leads to application (even if the application is not foreseen at the time), future adverse effects might result from any particular scientific activity. Accordingly, the developing countries express a strong interest in having either regulatory jurisdiction over scientific research conducted over their continental shelves or within a reasonable distance from their coasts, or a requirement of total, compulsory disclosure of all samples, data, and interpretation thereof as a matter of right.

In view of the virtual unanimity of research scientists in the United States on the needs of this interest group, how have they fared in the 1970–1971 proposals?

The first observation one must make is that there has been no specific US proposal concerned exclusively (or even primarily) with freedom of scientific research. Article 24 of the Draft Convention provides:

(1) Each Contracting Party agrees to encourage, and obviate interference with, scientific research.

(2) The Contracting Parties shall promote international cooperation in scientific research concerning the International Seabed Area:
    a. by participating in international programs and by encouraging cooperation in scientific research by personnel of different countries;
    b. through effective publication of research programs and the results of research through international channels;
    c. by cooperation and measures to strengthen the research capabilities of developing countries, including the participation of their nationals in research programs.

This obligation to obviate interference with scientific research applies to the International Seabed Area which constitutes the area seaward of the two hundred meter isobath. It does not purport to change the existing rules relating to the necessity for securing consent of the coastal state to conduct scientific research operations on the continental shelf.[40] Save for the "anti-creeping jurisdiction" concepts embodied in the Draft Convention,[41] the US Government has made no other proposals relating to freedom of scientific research which would modify the existing rule of Article 5 (8), nor has it included anything more than the most general statement reflected in Article 24 of the Draft Convention.

It would appear then that the scientific research community has fared rather badly as a special interest group. Perhaps this is due in part to the relative unimportance of scientific research in terms of short term economic product. It may also be due to the fact that the DOD opposes *specific* grants of freedom of access for pure scientific research on the grounds that this might somehow negate the rights of access for military research purposes on the high seas. Also, the marine science community certainly does not have the constituency, as noted earlier, to be an effective advocate in the current national oceans policy debate, no matter how articulate or skilled its advocates. For all of these reasons marine science has had nowhere near the impact on the Task Force that the Department of Defense, the oil industry, and the fisheries industry have had.

In any event, one must recognize that knowledge about the oceans is a sina qua non to all other uses and that it is therefore difficult to quantify the ultimate value of scientific research.

[40] Article 5 (8) of the Convention on the Continental Shelf provides:
The consent of the coastal State shall be obtained in respect of any research concerning the continental shelf and undertaken there. Nevertheless, the coastal State shall not normally withhold its consent if the request is submitted by a qualified institution with a view to purely scientific research into the physical or biological characteristics of the continental shelf, subject to the proviso that the coastal State shall have the right, if it so desires, to participate or to be represented in the research, and that in any event the results shall be published.

[41] See note 34 supra.

There are now a number of specific proposals circulating, some being funneled to the Task Force through the Marine Science Subcommittee of ACLOS, others through the National Academy of Sciences' Ocean Affairs Board and its International Marine Science Affairs Policy Committee, in an attempt to assist in the formulation of a US policy on this subject. Like fisheries, and in view of the fact that there are as yet no really meaningful US proposals in this area, it is conceivable that the scientific research community can have a significant role in policy formulation on this topic.

E. *Hard Minerals*

In spite of the fact that they are both mineral extractive industries, the position of the hard mineral mining industry differs in several respects from that of the oil industry. Like the oil industry, the hard mineral industry is interested essentially in an economically and politically stable regime for the conduct of its activities so that it can proceed with the business of maximizing profits from the exploitation of seabed minerals. Insofar as the geographic areas of interest are concerned, however, the hard mineral industry appears to have much more interest in the deep ocean floor where the greatest concentrations of the richest mineral bearing manganese nodules are located. Further, the mineral leasing provisions of the Outer Continental Shelf Lands Act (OCSLA hereinafter), particularly the requirement of competitive bidding,[42] are deemed unsatisfactory by the hard minerals industry, and it is doubtful the United States would extend its jurisdiction through the OCSLA to the deep seabed deposits in question.

---

[42] Outer Continental Shelf Lands Act, 43 U.S.C. §§1331–43 (1964) (originally enacted as Act of August 7, 1953, ch. 345, 67 Stat. 462). Section 8 (e) of that Act provides:

The Secretary [of the Interior] is authorized to grant to the qualified persons offering the highest cash bonuses on a basis of competitive bidding leases of any mineral other than oil, gas, and sulphur in any area of the outer Continental Shelf not then under lease for such mineral upon such royalty, rental, and other terms and conditions as the Secretary may prescribe at the time of offering the area for lease.

The Draft Convention would seem to offer satisfaction on both counts—a proposed regime to govern operations beyond the limits of national jurisdiction, and specific provisions favorable to hard mineral exploratory activities.

However, and unlike many of the other interests, the hard minerals industry has proceeded to express its preferences in a form other than the Executive Branch of the government, specifically by securing the introduction of S. 2801 and H.R. 13904 (92d Cong., 1st Sess., 1972) which envision a system of parallel national legislation by countries with advanced hard minerals technology to ensure protection of deep sea mining operations from competing claims of their own nationals.[43]

It is obvious that US policy expressed in the Draft Convention was not considered sufficient by the hard minerals industry for its near term interest. This is probably not due so much to dissatisfaction with the substance of the regime proposed as to the timing thereof. The industry suggests that it is unlikely that the Draft Convention or anything like it could be adopted sooner than 1974, but even if it were it could not become binding international law much earlier than 1980. The hard minerals industry is actively engaged in pilot projects and in at least one instance projects commercial operations by 1975. Security of tenure for formal prospecting activities, according to industry spokesmen, is needed now. This then is the reason for pursuing S. 2801 and H.R. 13904 in Congress.

At the same time, of course, the hard minerals industry is attempting to influence the substance of the Draft Convention or any other international agreement on seabed mining. This presents a novel and interesting situation—with one hand the hard minerals industry is making a serious effort through the Hard Minerals Subcommittee of ACLOS and other forums to

[43] Hearings on H.R. 13904 were held before the Subcommittee on Oceanography, House Committee on Merchant Marine and Fisheries, on 12 and 16 May 1972. For an excellent and detailed explanation of the proposed legislation and its potential effects see the statement by John G. Laylin, a Washington, D.C., attorney, delivered before the Subcommittee on Oceanography on 12 May. *Cf.* testimony of the author on the same date in opposition to the measure.

affect the Executive Branch's policy determinations on seabed mining. With its other hand, it is attempting to influence Congress to adopt legislation which might have unfortunate repercussions for the law of the sea negotiations being conducted by the Executive Branch.[44] Of course, this is a legitimate exercise of political power and indicates yet another method by which US oceans policy can be substantively influenced.[45]

F. *Transportation*

The needs of the maritime transportation industry can be stated quite simply: maximum mobility at the least possible

[44] In the testimony referred to in note 42 supra, the author suggested that enactment of S. 2801 or H.R. 13904 would constitute, in fact if not in form, an appropriation of deep seabed hard mineral resources by technologically advanced states contrary to the intent of General Assembly Resolution 2749 ["No State or person, natural or juridical, shall claim, exercise, or acquire rights with respect to the area or its resources incompatible with the international regime to be established and the principles of this Declaration."] and contrary to present US oceans policy. The result could be to precipitate unilateral claims by developing nations to two hundred mile (or possibly greater) "economic resource zones" in which they would assert exclusive rights to all living and nonliving resources, excluding international standards or machinery from the area. This result would be prejudicial to national security interests, several long range foreign policy objectives of the United States, and the development of a meaningful international order in the oceans. The author recommended that action on S. 2801 and H.R. 13904 be deferred at least until the Third United Nations Conference on the Law of the Sea has had an opportunity to meet and has failed to reach an acceptable agreement relating to mining of deep seabed hard mineral resources.

[45] Consideration of the role of Congress in oceans policy formulation has been deliberately omitted from this analysis. It should be noted, however, that Congress has from time to time asserted great interest in and even specified recommendations concerning US oceans policy. Through mid-May, 1972, two separate sets of hearings had been held this year alone in the House of Representatives (one by the Subcommittee on International Organizations and Movements of the Committee on Foreign Affairs, the other by the Subcommittee on Oceanography of the Committee on Merchant Marine and Fisheries) and hearings by the Senate Commerce Committee and the Senate Interior and Insular Affairs Committee were planned for later in the year. Of course, ultimate legislative oversight for any international agreement on ocean space will fall to the Senate Foreign Relations Committee whose Subcommittee on Ocean Space has in the past evidenced great interest in the subject.

cost. Among other elements in its position is objection to a plethora of differing regulations regarding pollution emanating from each separate national jurisdiction through which ships must pass, as well as to anti-pollution legislation which is restrictive to the point of prohibition.[46] Countering these perceived needs are the very real concerns expressed by some coastal states over the possible adverse effects stemming from activities of or accidents involving ships near their coasts. Clearly, Articles I and II are favorable to the maritime transportation industry since they facilitate passage through international straits and reduce the possibility of imposed costs which might prevail in a system of innocent passage. The maritime industry might also find some satisfaction in the provisions of the Draft Convention designed to limit or freeze national claims to jurisdiction over adjacent ocean areas (e.g., for pollution prevention regulations), although this is predicated upon the validity of the concept of creeping jurisdiction to which the DOD, but not many others, subscribes. The transportation industry also has a substantial stake in the regimes adopted concerning environmental protection, for decisions made concerning the problem of spillage of oil from large tankers as well as the intentional discharge of wastes can have substantial economic impacts on the maritime industry. It seems more appropriate, however, to discuss US policy on environmental questions in terms of the environmental interests.

In summary, since the interests of the transportation industry are quite similar to those of the Department of Defense (insofar as the latter is concerned with naval mobility), the industry has obtained relatively satisfactory results. It is to be observed, however, that it did so primarily on the coattails of the DOD, and not so much as a result of its own efforts to affect policy.

[46] This latter fear was generated principally by Canada's enactment of the "Arctic Waters Pollution Prevention Act of 1970" [18 and 19 Eliz. 2 C.47 (Can. 1970), reprinted in 9 *International Legal Materials* 543 (1970)] which imposes extremely strict regulations on vessels seeking to navigate the Northwest Passage and other Canadian waters. It has been argued that for all practical purposes, the Act prohibits oil tanker shipping in the Passage.

G. *Environmental Protection*

The perceived needs of those interested in protecting the marine environment are so obvious as to not need elaboration. Environmentalists generally acknowledge the need for developing energy and food resources from the ocean, but wish those operations conducted so as not to create any irreparable damage to the marine environment. This objective can be achieved through prohibition or extreme restriction on ocean dumping,[47] the limitation of offshore oil and gas drilling operations to the point of virtual assurance against major oil spills, the prevention of oil discharge and accidents involving large oil carrying tankers at sea, and sufficient regulations on the conduct of other activities in the ocean so as to prevent unacceptable levels of pollution. Some of these objectives (e.g., ocean dumping) will obviously require international agreements. Others (e.g., spillage from supertankers) may be achieved through expanded coastal state jurisdiction over potential pollution causing activities. An example of the latter approach is Canada's Arctic Waters Pollution Prevention Act of 1970.[48] Clearly the thrust of the Draft Convention and Articles I and II is away from this nationalistic approach. If, however, appropriate and adequate international agreements can be secured, environmental protection interests will still be served. One obvious consideration is speed—unilateral action can be swift, oriented specifically to the perceived threat, and therefore effective; international action is likely to

[47] The United States proposed an ocean dumping convention in connection with the UN Conference on the Human Environment held in Stockholm June 5–16, 1972. The Intergovernmental Meeting on Ocean Dumping held at Reykjavik, Iceland, April 10–15, 1972, also adopted "Draft Articles of a Convention for the Prevention of Marine Pollution by Dumping" [Doc. No. IMOD/2, 15 April 1972] which by resolution of IMOD was forwarded to the Stockholm meeting "for further consideration and appropriate action" [Doc. No. IMOD/3, 15 April 1972]. There are several important differences between the US approach and the draft articles adopted by IMOD. The Stockholm Conference did not deal specifically with the draft proposals but rather endorsed by resolution the idea of convening a plenipotentiary conference on ocean dumping before the end of 1972. The Conference also referred the matter to Subcommittee III of the UN Seabed Committee.

[48] See note 46 supra.

be slow in coming about, general in nature, and not necessarily responsive to new developments.

Another consideration is the level at which one attacks the problem. As pointed out by Jacques Piccard at the *Pacem in Maribus II* Convocation held in Malta in the summer of 1971:

> It is completely impossible to dissociate problems of the Mediterranean from those of the rest of the oceans. It is impossible to dissociate pollution in territorial waters from the pollution of international waters. It is also impossible to dissociate problems of the pollution of the sea from the problems of the pollution of the soil and of the atmosphere of our planet. It is impossible to dissociate the problem of pollution from the problem of population explosion. And, finally, it is impossible to completely dissociate the problem of population explosion from the problem of technical progress.[49]

Suddenly one finds oneself regulating the number of babies which a family can have in order to prevent pollution of the Mediterranean! The interrelationship is, of course, valid. On the other hand, it is necessary to attack the ultimate and specific results of technological advancement at the same time we are making the critical decisions about rates of growth both of industry and of population.

To date, US law of the sea initiatives concerning environmental protection have been primarily limited to two areas: (1) ocean dumping, in which the United States has submitted a draft convention, and (2) the Draft Convention provisions designed to limit or eliminate pollution of the sea resulting from the exploitation of the resources of the seabed and subsoil. Article 23 of the Draft Convention contains general provisions requiring the International Seabed Resource Authority to prescribe rules to ensure the protection of the marine environment. Clearly, the United States is not going to develop a unilateral

---

[49] Jacques Piccard, "The Pollution of the Mediterranean: Panel Statement," *Proceedings of Pacem in Maribus II*, p. 129 (1971).

approach to pollution control because of the Department of Defense oriented policy away from assertions of extended national jurisdiction over ocean space.

One serious problem to be considered by the US Government is the respective roles to be played by the Intergovernmental Maritime Consultative Organization (primarily concerned with spillage of oil from tankers), the UN Conference on the Human Environment (which has a comprehensive perspective), and the Seabed Committee (which is primarily concerned with prevention of pollution from the exploitation of the resources of the seabed and subsoil). In fact, the Environmental and the International Law and Relations Subcommittees of ACLOS have specifically been requested to submit suggestions concerning appropriate institutional structures for pollution prevention in the oceans.

The effect which the special interest group concerned with environmental protection in the oceans will have on the outcome of US policy depends in large part on the national policy positions being decided at the level of the Environmental Protection Agency and the Council on Environmental Quality concerning the balance between technological progress and protection of environmental values. The pollution of the ocean from tankers and from fixed installations for the exploitation of seabed resources is very small when compared to the pollution of the ocean from land based sources (including fallout from air pollution). Thus, if a global approach to environmental management is the goal of the environmental interests, it would seem more fruitful to work through the type of international environmental agency recommended to the General Assembly by the UN Conference on the Human Environment (UNCHE). (UNCHE's Declaration on the Human Environment is contained in Appendix V.)

To date, then, and insofar as the 1970–1971 law of the sea proposals are concerned, US policy seems to have taken adequate account of the need to condition seabed resource exploitation with reasonable rules for the protection of the marine environment, but beyond that level one moves rapidly into forums other than the Task Force and it is here that meaningful input will have to be made.

Summary

This analysis assumed a general disposition to permit special interests to have a major role in establishing US foreign policy. Many might disagree, pointing out that neither the oil industry nor the fishing industry nor the scientific research community nor anyone else should be able to prejudice the long range goals of this nation in the world because of short-term economic or other requirements. While there is merit in this view, it overlooks the fact that the range of interests in the ocean is so diverse—from extractive industries through scientific research, to environmental protection, and not excluding national defense —that it encompasses virtually the entire national interest.

With the creation of ACLOS, the US Government has taken a desirable step towards involving special interest groups in the formulation of oceans policy. How well that organization is utilized and how independent it is in its judgments are questions yet to be answered. Accordingly, no evaluation of its performance can be made at this time.

Substantively, there are special interests which clearly are not getting sufficient attention at the present time from policy makers framing US initiatives in the international law of the sea negotiations. On the other hand, there are certain interests —one thinks of the Department of Defense and the petroleum industry—which seem to be getting their perceived needs satisfied at the expense of others. The law of the sea debate involves difficult and complex problems of establishing goals, ascertaining values, and accommodating conflicting interests. Hopefully, the new administrative structure will in the future provide a more equitable balance among the diverse participants.

II

A LAW OF THE SEA CONFERENCE—
WHO NEEDS IT?[1]

ROBERT L. FRIEDHEIM

This chapter takes stock of the state of international negotiations on the law of the sea. It assesses the usefulness of the discussions in the UN Seabed Committee (constituted as the preparatory committee of the Law of the Sea Conference) not only as to whether there will be sufficient progress in them to justify a plenary Law of the Sea Conference in the near future but also as to what substantive direction the discussions seem to be taking. These questions have enormous implications. With the exception of certain problems relating to ocean use such as pollution, solutions to which will be negotiated in other international forums such as the Stockholm Conference on the Human Environment or the Intergovernmental Maritime Consultative Organization Conference, governments are relying almost solely upon a single, indefinite, universal lawmaking conference to resolve the multiple problems of the increased uses of the sea. Should the conference not take place or should it fail, the world may experience the anarchy on the seas that the headline writers are so fond of evoking.[2]

Unfortunately, the writers may have the opportunity to reuse the phrase if the results of the March 1972 preparatory meeting are accurate indicators of progress in the negotiations. There were, in fact, no major public signs of productiveness. The in-

---

[1] This paper was not produced as part of the author's work at the Center for Naval Analyses and the ideas expressed herein are his own. The paper does not necessarily represent the views of the Center, the United States Navy, or the United States Department of Defense.

[2] James P. Brown, "Anarchy at Sea," *New York Times*, 10 April 1972.

dicators pointed either to no progress or to some disquieting evidence of unresolvable conflict. Since the committee's work was conducted principally in subcommittees, the state of the negotiations can better be evaluated by reviewing what occurred in each subcommittee.

Subcommittee I, dealing with the seabed regime and machinery, a problem in which the United Nations has been involved since the 1967 Twenty-second General Assembly, engaged in further general debate on the subject.[3] Ideally, progress should have been made toward drafting a regime convention since there were a number of formal proposals on the table; but no draft came out of the subcommittee.

The situation in Subcommittee II was much worse. Although it was responsible for traditional law of the sea problems—territorial seas, straits, fishing—these subjects were relatively new to the Seabed Committee negotiations. The subcommittee never really considered the substantive problems. It was stalled almost to the last moment of its meetings waiting for the Group of 77 (a caucusing group of the developing states) to agree upon a list of subjects for the agenda. While it was annoying to the developed states to wait and waste valuable negotiating time while the developing states resolved their internal contradictions, they were stunned when the Group of 77 presented its list in the waning hours of the March session. The list stated some issues of high salience to developed states in such a prejudicial way that if the developed states had chosen to bring their concerns to the floor of the conference, they legitimately could have been ruled out of order by the chair. Their concerns

[3] The proceedings of the March 1972 meeting of the Seabed Committee can be followed in: United Nations General Assembly, Committee on the Peaceful Uses of the Seabed . . . Plenary Meeting, *Provisional Summary Records of the Seventy-First to Seventy-Seventh Meeting* (UN Doc. A/AC.138/SR.71–76) ; Sub-Committee I, *Provisional Summary Records of the Thirty-Second to Forty-Seventh Meeting* (UN Doc. A/AC.138/SC.I/SR.32–47) ; Sub-Committee II, *Provisional Summary Records of the Twenty-Fourth to Thirty-Second Meetings* (UN Doc. A/AC.138/SC.II/SR.24–32) ; Sub-Committee III, *Provisional Summary Records of the Fifteenth to Nineteenth Meetings* (UN Doc. A/AC.138/SC.III/SR.15–19) .

simply were not on the agenda. Obviously the list proved unacceptable to the representatives of the developed states.

The proceedings of Subcommittee III, established to deal with problems of ocean science and ocean environment, were almost entirely ineffectual, especially if one is concerned with problems of the environment. At its infrequent meetings many of the delegates complained that the Stockholm Conference (held in June 1972) was usurping their prerogatives. Aside from giving some developing countries' representatives the opportunity to complain that all ocean ecology decision making should have been transferred to Subcommittee III, which has no claim to expertise in environmental matters, there is little to report on the proceedings of the subcommittee. In short, on law of the sea subjects, some of which have been under continuous negotiation since 1967, we have reached a temporary stalemate.

Developed and developing countries have contributed equally to this impasse. Both will have to contribute to the removal of obstacles. Nevertheless, the impasse could have been avoided had the developed states adopted a more perceptive set of tactical policies. They should have been able to foresee the direction discussions were likely to take in the UN Seabed Committee and then to have acted accordingly. Instead, events were allowed to take their course.

Several reasons may be cited to explain the failure of the developed states and, in particular, the United States, to fully comprehend the problems involved in resolving ocean issues. Most important is misperception of the nature of the United Nations as an institution and, as a consequence of that misperception, of the politics of the law of the sea. If the developed states look realistically at the situation, perhaps the negotiations can be brought to fruition. By that is meant a situation where nations have identified actions which, if taken, would benefit both developed and developing countries.

The Politics of the Law of the Sea

For a fourth time in the twentieth century (the first three were the League of Nations Codification Conference of 1930, and the UN Law of the Sea Conferences of 1958 and 1960), the interested parties have brought law of the sea problems to what there is of a centralized world decision apparatus. As will be seen, this confidence in global lawmaking (i.e., all the states of the world sitting at a conference rationally making the perfect set of universally applicable rules, viable for our, if not all, times) has resulted in an overestimate of the ability of the UN General Assembly or a UN conference to act as a world legislature. Reliance primarily if not solely upon a universal conference has also had the effect of cutting off the search for alternate means of resolving the problems relating to future uses of the sea. It may ultimately be discovered that a UN conference is not the most appropriate or certainly not the only negotiating forum.

Regardless of the wisdom of the decision, the United Nations has been summoned for the third time to consider law of the sea matters. If a UN Law of the Sea Conference is to be successfully concluded, the political nature of the UN system must be understood.

Ascribing grandiose lawmaking functions to the United Nations obscures a fact that is well-known in relation to domestic legislatures—they are political institutions. Any problems they will handle—well or poorly—they will handle in a political manner. It must not be forgotten that the UN General Assembly is a political forum in which states and groups of states attempt to foster and protect what they believe to be their interests. The global community may be attempting to create law at the UN Law of the Sea Conference, but the problems that arise are more a result of clashing national wills on policy than of contrasting legal philosophies.[4] It must be recognized that the heart of the

---

[4] Obviously national will and legal philosophy are related, but the emphasis on law as the only legitimate set of governing rules is peculiarly a Western notion. Or, as Lucian W. Pye has put it ". . . the Europeans who restlessly moved out into the rest of the world [during the age of European imperialism] constantly felt there was something deficient in societies not governed by an explicit system of law." The very different culturally based perceptions of the role of law, and the superimposition of legal institutions and legal concepts on colonial areas by the West are matters not unrelated to the basic attitudes many non-Western states bring to the current law of the seas negotiations. For an excellent essay on how Western legal notions

debate on the law of the sea is the question of allocation—allocation of the ocean's areas and permissible uses between contending parties that consider notions of "jurisdiction," "control," or "freedom" not as theoretical abstractions, but as concepts which enhance their short run interests or provide them some tactical maneuver room.

Most of the developing states recognize this fact. Indeed they find it desirable. For them, the United Nations is a forum in which they can take action to overcome the disadvantages they suffer. Doubtless they find the United Nations a relatively weak institution, but given their individually insufficient capabilities, it is often the best means available to them in confronting the developed countries.

In contrast, too often the developed states have talked as if the schemes they propose concerning the law of the sea were purely altruistic, having nothing to do with their national interests and put forth entirely to protect the interests of the world community as a whole. In some respects, these assertions are correct. In other respects they are mere pretense—as the developing states claim. Such cynicism among the developing countries is justified if only because it is difficult for even the developed state sponsors to separate the self-serving from the altruistic. Whatever the reason now for projecting a selfless image, it was tried before and it failed. The developed states' legalism and idealism did not impress the developing countries in 1958 and 1960.[5] There is no reason to believe they will today.

Such a stance by the economically more advanced nations creates the wrong psychological climate for realistic bargaining with the developing countries. One of the reasons the states of the third world seem to be threatening to act completely without

———————

were grafted onto non-Western systems, see Lucian W. Pye, "Law as the Source of Both Instability and Rigidity," *Aspects of Political Development* (Boston: Little, Brown, 1966), pp. 113–125.

[5] For a discussion of the negotiating behavior in the 1958 and 1960 Law of the Sea Conferences, see: Robert L. Friedheim, "The 'Satisfied' and 'Dissatisfied' States Negotiate International Law: A Case Study," *World Politics* XVIII:1 (October 1965), 20–41.

regard to the interests of the developed countries is that it has not been conveyed clearly to them that negotiations cannot succeed unless the vital interests of *both* sides are taken into account.

The developing states control numbers; the developed states have real ocean capability. If ocean problems are to be solved in the UN context, compromise is indicated. Where positions are mutually exclusive, existing proposals must be dropped and alternatives found.

A second basic factor in assessing the United Nations as a negotiating forum is a recognition of how its General Assembly, or General Assembly-sponsored conference, without Charter reform or change, is permanently skewed in favor of the developing states. There is now a permanent majority of states from the third world in the General Assembly. In theory, if the developing countries can maintain sufficient discipline to marshal their votes, they can pass any resolution they please, however prejudicial to the minority of developed states. In other words, they are in a position to be rampantly majoritarian.[6]

At least three further observations must be drawn from this fact. First, the issues that will be negotiated seriously at the United Nations are those that are salient to the majority. Second, there will always be the threat of the exercise of majoritarianism throughout the negotiations. Third, the majority will not be interested in developing rules for the ocean divorced from extra-oceanic considerations. All three of these points overlap, but they can be separated somewhat for discussion.

If it is necessary to have issues on any UN agenda salient to the majority, it is essential to consider the question whether the law of the sea per se is salient to the developing countries. The answer is that the law of the sea as we know it is only indirectly relevant to the developing states. It is the ocean users—the developed states—who claim an imperative need for known rules

[6] On majoritarianism, or the tyranny of the majority, see: Robert A. Dahl, *A Preface to Democratic Theory* (Chicago: University of Chicago Press, 1956), and Henry Steele Commager, *Majority Rule and Minority Rights* (New York: Oxford University Press, 1943).

of transiting on, over, and under the ocean, who need laws to state with precision what the rules are governing ocean exploitation (fishing, oil, minerals), who are concerned with ocean science both as a source of useful information and source of scientific truth, and who, because they are both major offenders and major potential victims, wish to bring man's degradation of his environment under control.

While some developing states have substantial ocean interests (the West Coast Latin Americans in fishing, some African and Middle Eastern states in offshore oil), most are primarily concerned with the problems arising out of their own underdevelopment. Thus there are two foci to the ocean concerns of the developing countries. The first is the hope that they might harness the resources of the oceans to quickly overcome their grave disadvantages. The second is to prevent the advanced industrial societies from using the oceans to widen the gap between developed and developing states.

It would be difficult for even the most hardened "bloated capitalist" to object to the first goal—even when it is recognized that ocean resources, like anything treated as a panacea, will not result in a miraculous cure of the development problems of most southern hemisphere states. Unfortunately, the false lure of vast amounts of money for development assistance was the focus of developing states' concern over ocean matters when the seabed debates began in 1967–68. The speech of Malta's Ambassador Arvid Pardo which began the debates seemed to promise revenues of the order of $5 billion a year to the UN treasury and a UN development fund.[7] It was tempting, of course, to imagine all that money available independent of, say, a Russian or French refusal to pay its assessment or the parsimony or ideology of the US Congress. But the promised bonanza quickly proved chimerical.[8] Nevertheless, as a result of the Seabed Committee

---

[7] United Nations Doc. A/C.1/1515, November 8, 1967.

[8] This was a result of detailed consideration of the economic problems of deep seabed resources exploitation in a number of Secretariat studies. These were listed in *Ocean Affairs Bibliography, 1971,* Ocean Series No. 302 (Washington: Woodrow Wilson International Center for Scholars, 1971), pp. 161–

deliberations a number of developing states now are seeking in a more reasonable fashion to harness the sea in their development struggle. The idea of extracting revenue is still alive; and the hope of many developing states to create ocean exploration and exploitation capabilities is becoming one of the major themes of the debate. Such aspirations ought to be viewed sympathetically by the developed societies not only because it is the "right" thing to do but because unless the developing states find some salient issues in the debate over the uses of the sea, they will anticipate no profit from the conference decisions. Thus, they will have no incentive to be cooperative.

Unfortunately another focus of some of the developing states cannot be viewed so benevolently by the developed countries— the desire to block or slow down the access of the advanced industrial societies to ocean uses and resources. Some developing states have expressed the fear that the developed states will use access to ocean resources or control of ocean uses (e.g., military and transport) to at least perpetuate the development gap, and perhaps widen it. The ocean as an issue area allows those developing states inclined to play zero sum games the opportunity to try to mobilize the third world as a whole to delay, or perhaps even prevent, achievement of the minimum necessary conditions of order for exploiting or using the oceans. Such an occurrence could be disastrous. A zero sum game is one in which one player wins, the other loses.[9] It is understandable that such a course would be tempting to the developing countries; but such action would reduce oceans problems to a mere surrogate for the main issues of the conflict between developed and developing states. This is not to say that there is no reality to developing states' fears that, left unchecked, the developed coun-

---

187. Nevertheless, the idea of enormous sums that might be available for international purposes, while moribund, is not dead. John J. Logue recently has been advocating UN action on the seabed because it is "The Trillion Dollar Opportunity;" see John J. Logue, ed., *The Fate of the Oceans* (Villanova: Villanova University Press for the World Order Research Institute, 1971), pp. xvi–xxix.

[9] For the zero sum game concept see: Martin Shubik, *Game Theory and Related Approaches to Social Behavior* (New York: Wiley, 1964), p. 15.

tries cannot use access to ocean areas and resources to benefit themselves and thereby widen the discrepancies between the two sets of states. But to handle the problem in this manner is clearly to play a zero sum game. Only in the narrowest sense could the developing countries win. All, in fact, would lose. We have returned to the problem of majoritarianism.

The temptation must be strong for the current developing states' majority to try to break the many deadlocked issues in UN negotiations simply by insisting upon its own way. Reportedly, such was nearly the case at the presentation of the developing states' list of subjects at the end of the March 1972 meeting of Subcommittee II mentioned earlier. It was feared that the developing countries were prepared to vote in their list as the agenda, thus precluding discussion of the superpower-backed formula of "free transit" through straits and restricting discussion to "innocent passage."[10] Thus far, the developing states have not, as often predicted, abused their position. But it must be understood that the threat will be constantly present when the issues under negotiation are important to both groups. At the least it should be recognized that the one state-one vote formula has made the UN General Assembly a tool of the developing countries, and they have no intention of meekly ratifying the legal rules their competitors find valuable.

The style of the negotiations are also distinctive and perhaps congenial to the developing states while most uncongenial to the developed states. The negotiations are full of opportunities for noisy, bombastic debate; they are general and comprehensive in scope; and they are poorly prepared (e.g., there is nothing like the International Law Commission-prepared texts that formed the core of the conventions adopted in 1958). Moreover, not only are the discussions notably disorganized but they are so structured that the negotiations cannot deal with ocean problems as a set of technical problems, with the best technical means of regulating ocean uses as the paramount consideration

[10] United Nations Doc. A/AX.138/66, 24 March 1972.

in the minds of the negotiators and the best technical constructs used as guides to policy. Thus much of the academic literature on the problems of the sea is likely to be irrelevant in evaluating the outcome of the negotiations, even if valuable in evaluating the underlying nature of the problems. Scholars have bitterly complained of the lack of expertise on the part of the members of the Seabed Committee. Diplomats—especially from developing countries—have responded in two ways: first, with resentment that they are being considered, as P. V. J. Solomon, Ambassador of Trinidad and Tobago to the United Nations, put it, "a bunch of incompetents who do not know how to approach . . . [their] . . . problems, and never did know the importance of the seabed question;"[11] and second, with smugness realizing that they, not the experts, will determine the outcome on the issues, at least in the UN system.

A preference for expertise is characteristic not only of academic specialists of developed countries, but also of these countries' negotiators. Unfortunately, this is a recurring attitude. The records of the earlier conference, as well as the present Seabed Committee discussions, are filled with remarks by delegates of developed states on their preference to depoliticize the issues, to listen to the experts, to seek the perfect legal formula, and to differentiate the "diplomacy of the sea" from a "true law of the sea."[12] One may legitimately share such feelings, but they have to be weighed against political realities. The developed countries must either learn to adapt better to UN-style negotiations, or, alternatively, find a more advantageous milieu in which to bargain where expertise is more prevalent and where the negotiators can view man's interests in proper use of the oceans as the principal consideration in making their decisions.

---

[11] For the statements of Professors Brown and Goldie, and Ambassador Solomon's reply, see: Lewis M. Alexander, ed., *The Law of the Sea: A New Geneva Conference,* Proceedings of the 6th Annual Conference of the Law of the Sea Institute (Kingston: University of Rhode Island, 1972) , pp. 3, 157, 161.

[12] See note 5 supra, pp. 32–39.

Problems Arising from the Nature of Negotiations

Unfortunately, no one has written a general guide to the operational code of the UN General Assembly.[13] We know there is a particular mode of operation in the General Assembly; and it has been labeled "parliamentary diplomacy."[14] The limited number of works on the subject point to the blend of *parliamentary* features so familiar to Westerners—collegiality, debate, and voting—and *diplomatic* features such as state sovereignty and sovereign equality. This blend makes UN negotiations distinctive.

Their distinctiveness is evident in the triad of voting, sovereign equality, and sovereignty. The combination of voting on formal decisions and the principle of sovereign equality, which gives each state, large and small, the same vote, would appear to be precisely the set of characteristics needed to fuel rampant majoritarianism. But this condition is offset by the fact that General Assembly votes merely lead to recommendations to sovereign states which are not required to take any action that in their opinion violates the essential nature of their sovereignty. It can

---

[13] For the idea of operational code see: Nathan Leites, *The Operational Code of the Politburo* (New York: McGraw-Hill, 1951) .

[14] The discussion of parliamentary diplomacy that follows is based on: Dean Rusk, "Parliamentary Diplomacy—Debate vs. Negotiation," *World Affairs Interpreter,* XXVI (Summer 1955) , 121–138; Philip C. Jessup, "International Negotiations Under Parliamentary Procedure," *Lectures on International Law and the United Nations* (Ann Arbor: University of Michigan, Law School, 1957) , pp. 405–419; Thomas Hovet, Jr., *Bloc Politics in the United Nations* (Cambridge: Harvard University Press, 1960) ; John G. Hadwen and John Kaufmann, *How United Nations Decisions are Made* (New York: Oceans, 1962) ; Hayward R. Alker, Jr. and Bruce Russett, *World Politics in the General Assembly* (New Haven: Yale University Press, 1965) ; Robert O. Keohane, "Political Influence in the General Assembly," *International Conciliation,* No. 557 (March 1966) ; Jack E. Vincent, "National Attributes as Predictors of Delegate Attitudes at the United Nations," *American Political Science Review,* LXII:3 (September 1968) , 916–931; Fred Charles Iklé, *How Nations Negotiate* (New York: Harper and Row, 1964) , p. 222; Jack Sawyer and Harold Guetzkow, "Bargaining and Negotiation in International Relations," in Herbert Kelman, ed., *International Behavior* (New York: Holt, Rinehart and Winston, 1965) , pp. 466–520.

be argued, of course, that conference derived conventions, even though not ratified by a state, may bind it if the rules become part of customary international law. In any case, the United Nations has very few mechanisms available to force compliance even of weak states. The problem is further complicated if the recalcitrant state is a major industrial country or a superpower.

In recent years the consequence of the inability of the General Assembly to force obedience by unwilling states has been the necessity to rely upon consensus or near consensus decision making. That is, it has become a virtual requirement for the sponsors of a proposal to continue negotiations to the point where overwhelming support is forthcoming rather than stop the bargaining when they believe they probably have achieved the bare requisite majority needed for formal voting passage.

Unfortunately, the proposals at the forthcoming UN Law of the Sea Conference are likely to be put to a series of open votes. If this is the case, and at least near consensus is not achieved, not only is it doubtful that the measures will be implemented by those states that vote no, but that requisite two-thirds majorities will even form on many issues. Most major law of the sea issues are so contentious that if put to the vote prematurely (that is, before at least near consensus is achieved) the conference will fail. Equally unfortunate is the fact that the requirement of near consensus puts a premium on intransigence, leads to least common denominator solutions, and makes the negotiations tedious and laborious.

It is obvious that where consensus is needed, the most intransigent participant is at a negotiating advantage if he holds out for as long as possible. He may not obtain all he wants, but his utility is increased by refusing compromise. Delay alone may allow outside events to make the proceedings moot. Essentially this has been the strategy of many Latin American states in defense of their position on the two hundred mile territorial sea. They have dominated floor discussion and helped to prolong the debate both substantively and procedurally. Although they deny it, to block the conference might assist in making a "plurality of regimes" a recognized part of customary international law;[15] at a minimum, it creates time to erode the ninety vote majority the Soviet Union claims for a twelve mile territorial sea proposal.[16]

Political scientists may applaud a least common denominator outcome of a political debate because it is *a* solution. The fear of many ocean specialists, on the other hand, is that many solutions that could command a requisite majority at a UN Law of the Sea Conference might not even solve the problems of a rational allocation of ocean uses and resources; indeed, in some cases they might exacerbate the problems.[17] But until a better mechanism than a UN Law of the Sea Conference is found, political acceptability will have a stronger effect on the outcome of the proceedings than workability in the real world.[18]

Another characteristic of UN politics relates to the type of issues which, if consensus is not achieved, are likely to be forced to a vote. Many of the most contentious issues which could be brought to a vote in a law of the sea conference are highly visible issues with a large symbolic content. Especially sensitive are those issues which deal with aspects of territoriality—borders, jurisdictional rights, sovereignty. For example, if freedom of ocean science, which in the minds of most developed state au-

---

[15] The denial was by Alvaro de Soto of the Peruvian Mission to the United Nations in Lewis M. Alexander, ed., *The Law of the Sea: A New Geneva Conference,* p. 195.

[16] United Nations Doc. A/AC.138/SC.II/SR.14, p. 11, 18 August 1971.

[17] This is made clear in the remarks at the 6th Annual Law of the Sea Institute Conference; see Lewis M. Alexander, ed., *The Law of the Sea: A New Geneva Conference.*

[18] Or, as Mr. Lazar Mojsov, Ambassador of Yugoslavia, has put it: "People are already blaming the United Nations Seabed Committee for this failure. This blame is sometimes based on the size of this Committee, and on the representation on it of the small States which have their incomprehensive fears about the urgent needs of the great and technologically advanced powers. I must assure you that this blame does not lie with the Seabed Committee of the United Nations. We who are the members of this Committee are there, not looking at these matters in terms of a neutral approach to the future needs of mankind; we are there as the representatives of our governments, and we express the views of our governments. So we should lay the blame for failures now or in the future on the absence of the necessary political support by individual States toward a new international codification of the rules concerning the law of the sea." Ibid., p. 73.

diences has a positive connotation, correlates very highly with control of territory in the minds of representatives of many developing states, we ought to be warned that such a concept will have a difficult time gaining a requisite majority if brought to a vote.[19]

When issues are symbolic, there is a tendency for states to be rigid in their voting. And what is being debated at the Seabed Committee are exactly those symbol laden concepts by which states define themselves. Despite statements by representatives of the developing countries that Western derived international law is unjust, they find some aspects of that law highly relevant to their present status and future aspirations. Many of the developing societies are "new" states in the sense that they are highly concerned with the integrity of their borders and the legitimacy of their governments. Thus they find concepts of sovereignty and territoriality highly salient. Many older developing states, especially Latin American, who feel the disparity between their power and that of the United States remaining constant or even growing, are sometimes even more territorially conscious. Many have made substantial unilateral claims on ocean areas. In non-public negotiations, doubtless some representatives of developing states will indicate that they recognize not only that their claims may present substantial problems to other ocean users but that they will have difficulty in enforcing their claims even if unchallenged by the developed states. Nevertheless, there is virtually no way to induce them to vote for a retrenchment of national claims. They will vote for the symbols which help reinforce their seeming independence. Statements on the part of developed states' representatives that they "do not see much point . . . in accommodating mere symbolism" are as foolish as they are arrogant.[20] The developing countries are just as prone to view proposals of the developed countries

[19] Robert L. Friedheim and Joseph B. Kadane, "Ocean Science in the UN Political Arena," *Journal of Maritime Law and Commerce* 3:3 (April 1972), 473–502.

[20] Statement of Leigh S. Ratiner, in Lewis M. Alexander, ed., *The Law of the Sea: A New Geneva Conference,* p. 93.

as symbolic—as symbols of great power hegemony.[21] Many third world states are not in a position to resist the developed states in exercising what these consider to be pre-existing rights; many more do not want to create a major incident and do not intend to challenge the great powers. But there is no reason to believe when an issue is symbolic of national sovereignty or of resistance to developed state domination that many third world countries can be induced to vote for it.

A number of developing states, especially Latin American, have pointed out that their territorial definitions are an inherent part of their status as nations. No regime would survive long if it voted contrary to the national myth. On occasion, American diplomats, who have frequently used the same theme in past UN negotiations, are reminded that the United States is not the only state which must respond to public opinion. Perhaps it is true that some of the leaders and diplomats of developing states have deliberately whipped up the nationalism of their people on ocean issues. But this is moot. What is important is that these developing states have backed themselves into a position which admits of no retreat. If there is an adverse vote on their favorite proposals, their acceptance of the ensuing convention should not be expected. In summary, sensible solutions to ocean problems will not be obtained if symbolic issues are forced to a vote. Such action would be a prescription for disaster.

The question arises whether the United Nations is the most suitable forum for the consideration of law of the sea issues. Negotiating ocean use problems in a universal forum tends to universalize problems, many of which might be better handled at a bilateral or regional level.

Many ocean use problems are area-specific, or if biological, stock-specific. For example, environmental degradation is a gen-

---

[21] For well argued, full expositions of the fear of the superpowers see the papers of Ambassador Joao Augusto de Araujo Castro of Brazil: "The United Nations and the Freezing of the International Power Structure," *International Organization* 26:1 (Winter 1972), 158–166; "Environment and Development: The Case of the Less Developed Countries," *International Organization* 26:2 (Spring 1972), 401–416.

eral problem, but when examined with care turns out to be more severe where there is an enclosed or semi-enclosed sea rather than an open ocean. The measures needed to deal adequately with the problem will very likely differ from region to region. Unfortunately many of these regional or local needs are swept aside in the search for a formula that a great variety of states with different characteristics could support.

Many ocean problems are area-specific in another sense—they are *political* regional problems. Much of the turmoil of the contemporary law of the sea is a result of the Latin American two hundred mile claims. Latin American governments have made no secret of the fact that their quarrel is with the United States. That is, it is a regional or hemisphere problem which—if the United States had paid serious attention to it in the 1950s and 1960s, as some students of the controversy claim[22]—might have been settled years ago had there been recognition that it related essentially to resource and not territorial claims. It appears to many observers that the United States preferred to bring the problem to the United Nations in the hope of using the totality of states to force a retreat by an aberrant regional group. It has not worked that way. Indeed, it has had rather the opposite effect of transforming a regional into a universal problem. It has forced the Latin Americans to lobby vigorously for their position among the developing states in general. It has made them try to sell the two hundred mile zone as the only possible salvation of the developing states vis-à-vis the rapacious industrial societies. If they succeed in selling this position to the developing countries, there will be a serious problem indeed. This will not be merely a voting problem; it will be a problem menacing international relations. It is one thing to contemplate the exclusion of non-coastal state users of the sea from an area two hundred miles from the coasts of Latin American states where there is sufficient open ocean (except on the Caribbean side) ; it

[22] David C. Loring, "The United States-Peruvian 'Fisheries' Dispute," *Stanford Law Review* 23:3 (February 1971) , 391–453; Barry B. L. Auguste, *The Continental Shelf: The Practice and Policy of the Latin American States, with Special Reference to Chile, Ecuador and Peru* (Geneva: DROZ, 1960) .

is another sort of problem in the more crowded waters off the coasts of European and Asian states, or oceanic archipelagos.

Observers of UN politics are aware that not all of the trade offs and deals are made on the particular items on an agenda. It is not unlikely that African states, for example, will base their votes on a resolution concerning the environment offered by a Western state on how that Western state voted on a resolution to impose sanctions on Rhodesia. Interissue trading is well known. Unfortunately, its value as a bargaining device gets blurred at a UN special conference. Sometimes this prevents understanding and dealing with the real underlying issues.

Too often Western delegations to special UN-sponsored conferences have prepared for the issues on the agenda of that conference and little else. Indeed, they are usually authorized to bargain only on the items on the formal agenda. In other words they may consider trading an orange for an orange rather than an orange for an apple. This appears to have been the case in the instructions of the US delegation to the UN Conference on the Human Environment. The *New York Times* reported that the delegation was instructed to vote to prevent either the conversion of a voluntary international environment fund into a development fund or the augmentation of the UN goal of earmarking one percent of gross national product as aid to developing countries.[23] One further US action guaranteed an increase in the suspicion of the developing countries about US motives underlying its environmental concerns. The US delegation was instructed to vote against the principle of "additionality." That is, the US delegation was forced to oppose the notion that it is an obligation of the developed states to pay for any increased costs borne by a developing state by the addition of environmental controls to its development plans and programs. It is a wonder that this alone did not lead to a negotiating breakdown at Stockholm and is a tribute to the much maligned practical sense of developing state negotiators.[24]

If the same pattern prevails in the instructions of the US dele-

---

[23] *New York Times,* 22 May 1972.

[24] Claire Sterling, "U.S. Losing Argument With Poor Nations at Stockholm," *Washington Post,* 8 June 1972, p. A29.

gation to the Law of the Sea Conference, the US delegation will be instructed to offer a concession in one aspect of the law of the sea for a concession in another aspect of the law of the sea. This would be unfortunate, because it does not reflect the necessities of the bargaining environment. The developing states are not, as we have seen, primarily interested in developing a set of rules for ocean use per se. What they want is precisely an apple for an orange—a concession by the United States for development assistance, more attention on the part of the United States to the plans of UNCTAD (the United Nations Conference on Trade, Aid, and Development), or lower developed state tariffs on the products of developing countries. Until the developed states understand that they must make concessions on subjects of interest to the developing states unrelated, or peripherally related, to the law of the sea in return for developing state concessions on the law of the sea, we can expect little progress in the law of the sea or any other negotiations between North and South participants.

The UN political process, blending sovereign equality with sovereignty, has had another deleterious effect on the law of the sea negotiations—it has heightened the inability of the Assembly or Seabed Committee to reduce the issues to manageable proportions. We have seen how the developing countries have expressed concern over the preference of the developed states for expert preparatory groups, depoliticization of the issues, a set date for the Law of the Sea Conference to begin, etc. We also have touched on the drive of the developing states to present an agenda favorable to themselves. All of this has made it difficult to create an adequate preparatory structure for the law of the sea negotiations.

The developing states are not alone to blame for this situation. All manner of states—developing or developed—who felt excluded by a Seabed Committee that was less than a committee of the whole complained of the limited membership of the Seabed Committee.[25] All manner of states who felt their interests

____

[25] See, for example, Australia (United Nations Doc. A/C.1/PV.1782, November 1970; A/AC138/SR.52, March 1971) ; Greece (United Nations Doc.

were involved were unwilling to delegate preparatory work to experts, or small working groups, and complained of lack of representation of states or blocs with their particular needs or characteristics. The result is essentially consideration by the whole United Nations (each Seabed subcommittee is virtually a committee of the whole), consideration of the issues with no agenda, and consideration of the issues with few specific preparatory materials.

How complex and nearly chaotic the situation is can be best visualized by trying to think in matrix form. For example, let us take the developing states' list of subjects as an indicator of the range of the issues and therefore the complexities involved in finding solutions.[26] It includes 63 separate and distinct categories of major issues which include a large number of contentious sub-issues. Assuming there will be an average of three sub-issues in these 63 categories, the total of voting issues forming one side of the matrix will be 189. On the other side of the matrix are placed the participants, perhaps as many as 142 states (132 UN members plus 10 states that are members of a UN functional agency but not the United Nations itself) who will be entitled to vote. With a 189×142 matrix we can see that there will be 26,838 decision cells. Thus a participating state in planning its strategy for the conference must not only be concerned with what its policy will be on 189 issues, but it must also attempt to understand how its preferences can be blended with the intricate decisional strategies of enough other states to form majorities. It is an awesome task with or without a computer. The problem of complexity alone is a reason to express concern about the possibility of success of a law of the sea conference.

Where Do We Go from Here?

If viewed in perspective, lack of substantive progress at the last several law of the sea negotiating sessions may not neces-

---

A./C.1/PV.1786, March 1970); Denmark (United Nations Doc. A/C.1/PV.1794, March 1970).

[26] United Nations Doc. A/AC.138/66, March 1972.

sarily point toward a disaster in the law of the sea. However, it is now clear that there will be a disaster if the Northern states —East and West—push the Seabed Committee into decisions that many of its members are not yet prepared to make. If the major issues are brought to a vote, we should expect, on a number of them, that the states of the UN system will vote according to their symbolic values and under the pressure of the parliamentary group process. Then developed ocean user states may have to seriously consider making flag state arrangements for their exploitative activities,[27] and run straits and territorial seas with their commercial and military vessels in defiance of coastal state attempts to control passage. Reciprocally, developing coastal states may continue to lay claim to large ocean areas and comprehensive or sovereign rights. If this occurs, serious, perhaps violent, clashes are very likely to follow.

The stalemate allows all states time to reconsider their positions on the issues. The time is needed. Hopefully, states will use it creatively. Signs are emerging that some of the developing states are growing in sophistication concerning ocean use issues. Recent proposals for enlarged national responsibilities emphasize more functionally specific controls related to particular problems such as economic zones or patrimonial seas. Some developing states seem to be demonstrating more willingness to give up general purpose or sovereign controls over activities not directly related to the coastal state claim, such as transit or overflight of a resource zone.[28] They also show a greater recognition that the coastal state will actually have to accept greater responsibilities and costs as a result of greater ocean use, and that real responsibilities will be a consequence of making a successful claim. There are also signs that some developing states are aware that they are better off creating a deep seabed ocean regime which gives a developed state exploiter some security of tenure in return for

[27] For an explanation of such flag state schemes see: Robert L. Friedheim, "Understanding the Debate on Ocean Resources," *Monograph Series in World Affairs,* University of Denver 6:3 (1969), p. 6.

[28] For a clear statement of this position, see the remarks of Mr. Kaniaru of Kenya in United Nations Doc. A/C.1/PV.1852, January 1972.

putting him under international controls. Thus some developing states recognize that if pushed far enough, as in the case of the developing state scheme to impose production controls on ocean minerals so that they would not compete with raw materials produced in developing countries, developed states might prefer to go to a flag state scheme of licensing.

Frankly, the stalemate gives all participants with important interests at stake time to back away from the extreme positions they so bravely announced on the floor of the Assembly or Committee. Many states—of greatly varying persuasions—doubtless would be grateful not to have to push the more symbol-laden issues to a vote.

The time gained in not trying to push a law of the sea conference too early to the voting stage will provide opportunity for a number of other important tasks. First among them is the task of seeking solutions to ocean use problems by means other than a universal UN-sponsored lawmaking conference. This may occur in two ways depending upon the circumstances. The first is by way of a *rival* medium for solving ocean use problems; the second is by way of a *supplement* to the UN proceedings.

One reason for the current impasse is that many of the participants did not understand the alternatives in the case of a breakdown in the law of the sea negotiations. The explanation for this is that the developed states never really considered an alternative to UN bargaining on a transnational, regional, or interested parties basis. Therefore they did not communicate to the developing countries that there existed an alternative in case of failure or intransigence.

The developing countries have not neglected such specialized conferences, with the Latin Americans meeting on law of the sea matters at Lima, Peru, and Montevideo, Uruguay; the Asian-African Legal Consultative Committee meeting at Colombo, Ceylon; and the heads of state or governments of non-aligned countries meeting at Lusaka, Zambia.[29] They have used such

---

[29] *Texts of the Montevideo Declaration-Lusaka Declaration . . . Report of the Subcommittee on the Law of the Sea of the Asian-African Legal Consultative Committee* (United Nations Doc. A/AC.138/34, April 1971) .

meetings to consolidate their bargaining position rather than as arenas in which to adopt their final positions. Nevertheless, if the Law of the Sea Conference does not convene, or fails, many of the developing states will try to enforce as law the positions they decided at such meetings.

The developed states should do no less, if only to demonstrate what would occur if there is no effort to reach compromise at Geneva. Moreover, given the technical resources available to the developed countries, specialized conferences can take the lead in drawing up the draft conventions which could then be presented either as documents the participating states alone would agree to or as the basis of further bargaining between the participating and nonparticipating states.

The second reason to look to regional, user, or specialized conference means of coping with new ocean use problems is that, even if the Law of the Sea Conference succeeds beyond expectations, it cannot deal with all relevant problems which need regulation. It cannot, first, because of sheer complexity of the issues; and second, because some problems are a result of local or regional physical or biological anomalies which should appropriately be dealt with on a less than universal level. Many intergovernmental organizations have interests in the oceans and have made important contributions to their better use.[30] They should be more frequently used, improved, and strengthened. Moreover, there is a warren of transnational nongovernmental organizations (the full range of which is not yet known) interested in the oceans whose services are available to help solve ocean problems.[31] There is no point in neglecting that which is not dramatic or instantaneous.

[30] Robert L. Friedheim, "International Organizations and the Uses of the Oceans," in R. J. Jordan, ed., *Multinational Cooperation: Economic, Social, and Scientific Development* (New York: Oxford University Press, 1972), pp. 223–281.

[31] For the concept of transnationalism see: Robert O. Keohane and Joseph S. Nye, Jr., eds., "Transnational Relations and World Politics," *International Organization* XXV:3 (Summer 1971), pp. 329–758. For an application of the theory to ocean affairs see Edward Miles' essay "Transnationalism in Space: Inner and Outer," at pp. 602–625 in the above volume.

Some of the time provided by the stalemate and consequent necessity for long, slow, and laborious bargaining should be expended in reexamining the fundamental issues of ocean use. Obviously, as ocean uses increase and selected ocean areas get congested, the old conceptual framework of freedom of the seas will become more inadequate. It is no longer sufficient to assume that any ocean user can do what he pleases as long as he does not interfere with the rights of others, because it is now known how interrelated are the activities on the oceans and how comparatively fragile the ocean is. Straits can be congested, offshore waters can be polluted, and the known fish stocks can be overharvested. In short, nations must deal with the problems arising out of the common property nature of the ocean. At the same time, the solution is surely not to extend national jurisdiction out to some midocean median point where one state's ocean territory will meet that of another state whose land territory begins on the other side of the ocean. "Balkanizing" the oceans, by reducing ocean territory to national property, may solve some problems but it may also give rise to other and more difficult ones. Some aspects of the traditional principle of freedom of the seas are clearly still relevant to the present and future rational and equitable use of the oceans. Somehow, the restrictions necessitated by greater use must be balanced with the freedoms that would allow mankind to use the oceans without excessive costs and administrative burdens. What is needed is a new operational concept for characterizing permissible future uses of ocean space.

III

NEW APPROACHES TO CONTROL OF OCEAN RESOURCES[1]

LEWIS M. ALEXANDER

The resources of the world ocean are a subject of strong and continuing debate both as to the estimates of their total value, and as to the organization or organizations which should have jurisdiction over them. Traditionally, ocean resources have been divided into two main categories—living and nonliving. The living resources are renewable, providing their harvest is kept within biological limits. Many of these resources are migratory, often moving throughout their lifetime over large distances. Nonliving resources are not renewable, and for the most part are fixed in place, thereby requiring different forms of management regimes than apply to living organisms.

In terms of jurisdiction, there are four types of regimes which might be established over ocean resources. First the resources could belong exclusively to the coastal state; it would then be the state's option to harvest them as it saw fit, to leave them undisturbed, or to permit nationals of another country (often under leasing or licensing arrangements) to partake of the exploitation. Alternatively, the ocean resources could be free to the use of all countries; in this case the resource would belong to him who first harvested it. Between these two extremes are the other alternatives. The resources could belong to some world authority, which would set out the guidelines for their acquisition and receive all or a portion of the wealth derived therefrom. Or they might become the property of a specific group of nations—possibly some sort of a regional bloc. This suprana-

[1] Nothing that appears in this article reflects in any way a policy position of the Law of the Sea Institute.

tional group could regulate the harvest, and the proceeds from the exploitation could be divided among the member countries or be acquired by the organization itself.

In addition to the harvest of living and nonliving resources the oceans also have other uses. They are of value as highways for commerce, as sites for oceanographic research, as media for the operation of military vessels. Equally important, they can be used as disposal areas for all manner of wastes, some of which may represent serious forms of pollutants. Along with the problems of jurisdiction over the harvesting of living and nonliving resources, it is important that some forms of control be placed when necessary on these other types of uses as well, in order that the oceans may be exploited wisely for the greatest good to the greatest number of people.

Types of Ocean Resources

Of living resources of the ocean, the most common form are the fish, which, for the most part, are migratory, but which tend to concentrate in certain geographic areas at certain stages of their life cycle. Some ocean areas are particularly valuable as fishing grounds; among these are the Grand Banks off eastern Canada, the North Sea, the coastal waters off Peru, and the northwest Pacific adjacent to Siberia and Japan. It is estimated that about 94 percent of the world catch of fish comes from within two hundred miles of land. Tuna and billfish are among the principal species taken from beyond that limit.

In the years since World War II the world catch of fish has gone up considerably. In 1948 it was seventeen million metric tons, and in 1968 it totaled sixty-four million tons. But in recent years the rate of annual growth has declined. The 1969 world catch of sixty-three million tons was one million less than in 1968, while in 1970 it rose again by six and a half million tons.[2] By 1985 the catch is expected to have increased over the 1970 figure by less than forty percent. The ranking of countries in

---

[2] United Nations, Food and Agriculture Organization, *Yearbook of Fishery Statistics, 1970* (Vol. 30) (Rome, 1971), p. 5.

terms of annual catch has also changed. The six leading producers in 1956 were Japan, United States, China, Soviet Union, Norway, and Peru in that order, while in 1970 they were Peru, Japan, China, Soviet Union, Norway, and the United States. The total volume of catch by the United States has remained almost the same for over thirty years although the consumption of fish and fish products has grown rapidly. In 1959 this nation produced 61 percent of its needs domestically, and imported 39 percent; in 1969 the figures were 36 and 64 percent respectively.[3]

Two types of fishing fleets—coastal and distant water—are involved in harvesting the sea's living resources. Coastal fishermen tend to stay close to land, often engaging only in day fishing. The fishermen are generally not mobile, and as long as they are based in one port are dependent on the resources within a limited area. Most of the world's fishing vessels belong to this category. But there are also the distant water fleets, which tend toward highly efficient harvesting techniques, and which travel hundreds or thousands of miles in search of their catch. The Soviet Union, Japan, the United Kingdom, West Germany, and Poland are among the countries with highly developed distant water fleets.

Most of the US fishing effort is carried out by coastal vessels, some of which—particularly in the northwest Atlantic and the northeast Pacific—are forced to compete with the distant water fleets of the USSR, Japan, Poland, and other countries. But the United States also possesses an efficient and highly capitalized distant water tuna fleet, as well as a less capitalized fleet of distant water shrimp vessels which travel through the Gulf of Mexico and Caribbean and down along the northeast coast of South America. Ideally the coastal water fishermen would prefer their government to proclaim exclusive rights over fisheries resources out to a considerable distance from shore, while the distant water fishermen would press for the right to fish as closely as possible to foreign coasts.

[3] U.S., Department of Commerce, National Oceanic and Atmospheric Administration, National Marine Fisheries Service, *Fisheries of the United States, 1971* (Washington, 1972), p. 34.

One of the basic elements in the composite of ocean resources —whether they be living or nonliving—is that of national expectations of the ultimate wealth to be derived from the resource use. There are two components: first, what is the estimated worldwide potential of the resources; and second, what share of the total wealth can a particular country reasonably expect to acquire?

Estimates of the total potential world catch of fish have tended to decline as greater knowledge of the stocks is obtained. A few years ago it was predicted that by utilizing traditional species, and with known techniques, it should be possible to realize an annual harvest of some two hundred million metric tons (of which less than a quarter was then being taken). But the most recent Food and Agricultural Organization estimate places the potential at one hundred million metric tons or less, or about half again as much as the current world catch.[4] The potential for tuna, shrimp and certain other species is considered good. In addition, the full exploitation of such types as squid, lantern fish and krill might add another eighty to one hundred million tons to the world annual total. But new knowledge, new techniques, and new markets must be found if a major expansion of the world fish catch, comparable to that of the past twenty years, is to take place within the next decade or so. Failing this, competition and congestion will grow increasingly severe as more and more countries build up their fishing effort and as those already involved in the harvest continue to increase their investment in their fishing capabilities.

Not all the living resources of the sea are composed of freely moving fish. There are also the sedentary or quasi-sedentary species, such as clams, oysters, lobsters, crabs, and scallops; as well as seaweed and kelp which are renewable and of considerable value within certain cultural groups. The living resources of the continental shelf—that is, those which at the harvestable stage are immobile on or under the seabed, or are unable to

---

[4] United Nations, Food and Agriculture Organization, *Atlas of World Fisheries* (Rome, 1971).

move except in constant physical contact with the seabed or subsoil—belong exclusively to the coastal state. These resources include clams, oysters, mussels, and (according to US definition) king crabs. But lobsters, scallops, and shrimp do not fall within this category, and are free for the taking by all coastal states' nationals beyond the exclusive fisheries limit. This complicated division of shelf species may before long be abandoned so that all living organisms associated with the seabed of the continental shelf will belong to the adjacent coastal state.

Of the nonliving resources by far the most important is oil. About seventeen percent of the world's oil production comes from offshore wells.[5] While a large proportion of these are located in the shallow waters of the Persian Gulf or Venezuela's Lake Maracaibo, there is still a substantial amount coming from the North Sea, southern California, and—increasingly—Southeast Asia. Estimates indicate that by 1980 some one-third of the world's oil may be coming from offshore production.[6] At present commercial exploitation comes from water depths of less than four hundred feet, but capabilities are expected before long to extend to considerably greater depths. Along with oil, natural gas is an important offshore product, particularly in the North Sea area. From the shallow waters of the Gulf of Mexico comes sulphur—also reclaimed from the subsoil by means of drilling.

The hard minerals lying on the seafloor are of three types. First are the sand, gravel, and oyster shell which are dredged from shallow waters near the coast. Second are the placer deposits—sediments washed down from the land—which contain gold, tin, platinum, diamonds, chromium, and other minerals. These deposits also are taken from shallow offshore areas, after

[5] M. B. Schaefer, "The Resources of the Seabed and Prospective Rates of Development as a Basis for Planning for International Management," in Lewis M. Alexander, ed., *The Law of the Sea: The United Nations and Ocean Management* (Kingston: University of Rhode Island, 1971), p. 89.

[6] W. H. van Eek, "Technology and Prospects for the Use of Areas and Mineral Resources of the Sea-bed and its Subsoil," *Symposium on the Exploration and Exploitation of the Sea-bed and its Subsoil* (Strasbourg: Council of Europe Consultative Assembly, 1970), p. 8.

which the heavy minerals are extracted from the sands. Finally there are the chemical precipitates of the deep ocean floor, particularly the manganese nodules, containing manganese, copper, tin, and cobalt; as well as the phosphorite nodules. These are not as yet commercially exploited, but before long technological advances should make their recovery economically feasible.

In addition there are the minerals contained within seawater, of which only magnesium and salt are now recovered commercially but which in the future could serve as important supplements to land based supplies particularly with respect to such products as sulphur, potassium, zinc, iron, and aluminum.

Existing Juridical Regimes

National jurisdictions in the ocean are based on two criteria: (1) codified international law particularly as expressed in the four Geneva Conventions of 1958; and (2) customary international law as it has evolved over the years. In general coastal states exercise sovereignty over a territorial sea up to a maximum distance of twelve nautical miles from their coast, subject only to the right by foreign vessels to innocent passage through territorial waters. At present some fifty-five countries claim twelve miles, forty-six claim breadths between three and twelve, while sixteen claim territorial seas greater than twelve miles in extent, of which nine claim two hundred miles.[7] And of those countries claiming less than twelve miles as the breadth of their territorial sea, twenty-four exercise exclusive jurisdiction over fisheries in the zone between the outer breadth of their territorial waters and the twelve mile limit off their coasts.

A second offshore boundary is that on the seabed. According to the Geneva agreements a coastal state exercises sovereign rights for exploring and exploiting the natural resources of its continental shelf extending out to the two hundred meter isobath (657 feet) or beyond "to where the depth of the superjacent waters admits of the exploitation of the natural resources

[7] See Appendix II for a complete tabulation of territorial sea claims.

of the said areas."[8] To date no country has claimed jurisdiction over the seabed beyond the two hundred meter depth on the grounds of its ability to exploit the resources, but the time for such claims may not be far off. If one country demonstrates its ability to exploit to a depth, say, of one thousand meters, and thus justifies its claim to jurisdiction to that depth, presumably all other states would have the right to extend their control to a similar depth off their own coasts.

Beyond these boundaries of national jurisdiction are the high seas which are free to the use of persons from all countries. Freedom of navigation, overflight, fishing, and scientific research are features of the high seas, with such profits as are involved accruing to those who carry out the operations. These freedoms, obviously, are of particular benefit to states with well developed maritime industries which can utilize the oceans to the best advantage. For many of the developing countries high seas' freedoms may be viewed as being to them of only limited advantage.

Impending Changes in Ocean Regimes

We are now in the process of preparing for a new Law of the Sea Conference which will reconsider, and probably rewrite, many of the 1958 Conventions. At this new conference the number of delegations may number well over 130, meaning that a two-thirds majority in support of any new proposal in plenary sessions may require as many as ninety supporting votes. So the questions arise, first, what sort of new regimes for ocean resources may get the required support for adoption; and second, what happens if the new Law of the Sea Conference fails to adopt any new regime at all?

As the law of the sea has gradually been evolved over past decades, a dominant theme, pressed forward by the United States, Japan, the West European states, the Soviet Union, and certain other countries, has been that of maximizing the freedom of the seas in terms both of geographic extent and of the

[8] *United Nations Conference on the Law of the Sea: Convention on the Continental Shelf,* UN Doc. A/CONF.13/55 (1958), Article 1.

activities which are unrestricted in areas beyond national limits. True, there have been disagreements between advocates of the three and twelve mile territorial seas, and between those favoring and those opposed to "closed" coastal water bodies such as bays and gulfs. But the essential principle of the freedom of the seas dominated the 1958 Geneva Conference and its successor in 1960.

But times have changed. Since the 1960 Conference over fifty countries have become independent, and even some of those which earlier had achieved self-rule are now increasingly unwilling to follow the lead of the developed maritime nations in retaining traditional rules for the law of the sea. These countries wish to protect the ocean resources off their own coasts beyond the twelve mile limit, even though by extending national jurisdiction seaward they may be jeopardizing freedom of transit, particularly by military vessels, and freedom of scientific research by foreign nationals.

This trend toward expansion of national competence into offshore waters may take either one of two forms. A coastal state may seek to extend its jurisdiction over water areas out to a considerable distance beyond the twelve mile limit. It may claim that the waters beyond twelve miles now form a part of its territorial sea; or the country may merely assert that it has exclusive rights to the resources—particularly fish—within these waters out to some distant boundary, possibly two hundred nautical miles from shore. The coastal state may be entirely lacking in the capacity to harvest the living resources itself out to that distance, or even to patrol the waters against foreign intrusion. But the government may feel that it should establish the right to lease the fisheries in these coastal waters to foreign nationals, thereby deriving a portion of the wealth from the harvest.

A second form of extension of national control involves the ocean floor. As noted earlier a state has exclusive rights to explore and exploit the natural resources of the ocean floor out to a depth of two hundred meters. This two hundred meter isobath lies close to the coast in some areas, and hundreds of miles offshore in others. The average distance from shore, worldwide, is forty-two nautical miles. According to the Geneva Convention, coastal state rights to the seabed and subsoil resources have had no effect whatever on the status of superjacent waters, thus upholding as much as possible the freedom of the seas doctrine. But two questions for the future arise. First, what arrangements will eventually be made for seafloor jurisdiction beyond the two hundred meter depth? Under what real world conditions will coastal state sovereignty be extended beyond that isobath? Secondly, for how long can the neat distinction between resources of the seabed and those of the superjacent waters be maintained? The distinction was enunciated by the major maritime powers before and during the First Geneva Conference in order to suit their peculiar interests, but in an age of increasing nationalism on the part of the developing countries, the distinction may soon be swept away.

Within the past five years a new component has entered the ocean resources debate—namely the possibility of a world authority managing ocean resource development beyond the limits of national jurisdiction. Already the United Nations has acknowledged that these deep ocean resources are the common heritage of mankind, and there is strong sentiment in the United Nations that a portion of the wealth derived from their exploitation should go to developing countries. Leaving aside the details of how an international mechanism will carry out this resource management, we are still faced with the questions, which resources will be affected by an international funding scheme, and—more important—where are the limits of national jurisdiction beyond which the international authority would prevail?

Let us consider these questions first from the standpoint of the ocean floor. Presumably all coastal states will continue to enjoy exclusive rights to the natural resources of the seabed and subsoil out to a depth of two hundred meters as provided for in the 1958 Convention. But already some coastal countries would like to see a distance equivalency provided—that is, their legally defined shelf should extend to a depth of two hundred meters, or out to fifty (or perhaps one hundred) miles from shore, whichever criterion gives them the greatest extent of sea floor within national limits. This concept of a distance equivalency is gaining considerable support in the United Nations.

Seaward of a country's shelf is the continental slope, where depths plunge more rapidly toward the abyssal floor. Near the foot of the slope there is generally a broad, gently sloping apron of sediments brought down from the shelf and slope. This continental rise may extend a considerable distance out onto the deep ocean floor. Like the shelf and slope it may also contain important oil resources. Presumably in the coming years these areas beyond the two hundred meter isobath will be the ones which are first exploited, and from which revenues may be derived for any projected international fund. So the question then comes up, will the shelf and slope eventually pertain to the coastal state, once the ability to exploit their resources has been accomplished? Should the limits of national jurisdiction be placed at the outer edge of the shelf, or somewhere else close to the shore? The answer depends on what the prevailing national interests of the world's states are. There are in the world today 148 independent states (including Rhodesia and Bangladesh) of which 30 are landlocked and 118 are located on the coast. One hundred and thirty of these (including 25 landlocked states) are members of the United Nations.

For the thirty landlocked countries and for some twenty-three others whose continental shelves abut on those of their neighbors so that no slope or rise exists, it would seem that their national interests lie in maintaining the limits of national jurisdiction close to the coast so that the revenues derived from exploiting the resources off someone else's coast will go to an international fund, from which the landlocked or shelf-locked country may derive some benefit. This group might be joined by about a dozen other countries bordering on the open ocean which have small areas of shelf and slope. But for well over half the countries of the world (most of them developing) which have some hope of acquiring revenue directly from the exploitation of seabed resources beyond the two hundred meter depth, the prospects of turning a portion of the anticipated revenue over to an international fund for the benefit of other countries is not an exciting one.

The United States, two years ago, suggested a compromise arrangement,[9] under which the exclusive rights of the coastal state to the seabed and subsoil resources off its coast would extend out to the two hundred meter isobath, but that beyond that point, down along the slope and upper portions of the rise, there would be a "Trusteeship Area" within which the seabed resources would belong to an international authority. Only the nationals of the coastal state, or their lessees, would be permitted to exploit these resources, but they would do so under general rules laid down by the authority. A portion of the revenue derived from such exploitation would go to the international fund. This proposal is now before the Seabed Committee of the United Nations.

The debate over where the outer limits of national jurisdiction should be on the sea floor shows little signs of settlement at this time. Yet some accommodation must eventually be reached if the concept of an international authority (to which most countries subscribe) is to be implemented. Failing agreement on a new seabed regime, the existing Geneva Convention would presumably still apply, and nations will be free to expand their control over the resources of the seabed beyond the two hundred meter isobath on the grounds of exploitability.

Turning now to fisheries the question of jurisdiction assumes new dimensions. An important part of the problem here is the conflict between coastal state and distant water fishermen—an issue which does not as yet exist with respect to the seabed. There is less pressure for a portion of the revenues derived from fishing beyond national limits to be turned over to an international fund, although in time such pressures may grow. Because of their migratory nature, fish do not lend themselves so readily to control by establishing a fixed-distance-from-shore boundary. Finally, there is, I think, need for some correlation

---

[9] *United Nations Draft Convention on the International Seabed Area,* UN Doc. A/AC.138/25 (August 3, 1970); see summary in Appendix III to this volume.

between the boundaries of national jurisdiction on the seabed and those within the water column.

In planning for any exclusive or quasi-exclusive fisheries zone beyond twelve miles from shore, a first point is that it should *not* acquire the status of the territorial sea. For one thing this status may preclude the passage of many types of ships and aircraft; for another the new status may affect the jurisdiction of the ocean floor beneath the affected waters. It would seem to be in the international interest to restrict the maximum breadth of territorial seas to twelve miles.

An extra-territorial fisheries zone might be justified, first, on the grounds of conservation and of rational exploitation of the resources. Rather than wait interminably for international fisheries' bodies to establish needed conservation regulations beyond territorial limits, it might be wiser for the coastal state to be empowered to enact the necessary rules, subject to some form of appeal by the affected foreign fishing interests. Moreover, within such a zone the coastal state might also be authorized to lay down restrictions governing the conditions under which fishing may be carried out, thereby avoiding unnecessary congestion, gear conflict, and the use of excessive fishing effort.

It is important that within this extra-territorial zone the special interests of the coastal fishermen of the coastal state be protected, perhaps by granting them a guaranteed quota of the total catch of preferred species. In this way they can avoid being overwhelmed by the greater harvesting capacities of foreign distant water fleets. Within this fisheries zone it may also be possible for the coastal state to realize additional wealth through the issuance of licenses to foreign fishermen operating within these waters.

But there are three other aspects to this problem. One is that within such an exclusive or semi-exclusive zone foreign fishermen should also be permitted to operate, particularly in respect to those species which are not entirely harvested by the coastal state nationals. Second, the foreigners should not be charged exorbitant fees for their licenses to fish in this zone; otherwise all or most of them will be effectively excluded. Finally, the establishment of an extra-territorial fisheries zone should not interfere unduly with other uses of the sea in this area, particularly the freedom of transit and overflight, and of scientific research.

It is for these latter reasons that some countries have suggested national jurisdiction over fisheries beyond territorial limits on the basis of stocks of fish, wherever these stocks are found, rather than on the basis of fixed distances from shore. For example, the United States might have exclusive rights over haddock and cod stocks off New England, no matter how far offshore these may be found; and if the United States begins to build up its harvest of pollock or other underutilized types, then these too should appertain to the United States to the extent that its own fishermen are able to harvest the stock. This species approach also envisions international control over widely ranging pelagic species such as tuna.

Many other countries are wary of this approach and prefer instead to think of a "patrimonial sea" or extra-territorial resource zone, in which the coastal state has exclusive rights to the harvest. Under one guise or another some governments are already talking about such a zone as extending up to two hundred miles from shore. If adopted universally, this extension, as noted earlier, would place all but six percent or so of the world's catch within national limits. Little has been said about whether or not within this proposed zone any part of the revenue from the catch would go to some form of international fund.

Alternative Arrangements for Ocean Resource Management

The problem of jurisdiction over marine resource use has been shown to involve both the ocean floor and the superjacent water column. Included in the jurisdictional question are three principal interest groups—the coastal state, the foreign states which may wish to exploit off its shore, and the international community representing both the landlocked countries and those coastal ones which desire a more equitable share of the wealth from the harvest of the ocean's resources. How can these diverse interests and conditions be accommodated?

One solution, as advanced by Malta's Dr. Arvid Pardo, is to establish a universal two hundred mile belt of "ocean space" off each country's coast, applying both to the water areas and to the seabed and subsoil.[10] Between one hundred and two hundred miles from shore, according to his proposal, a percentage of the revenue derived from resource exploitation would be contributed to an international fund. But a universal two hundred mile limit seems to some people an over-simplistic approach to what is a very complex problem. What effects would a two hundred mile limit have on jurisdiction over the continental shelves, slopes and rises of the world? What chance would the landlocked and shelf-locked countries have of participating in resource exploitation? Regardless of Pardo's suggested text, what freedoms would in fact remain within the two hundred mile zone after a few years?

It is for these reasons that some alternative solutions should be considered. Let us start with the seabed. The exclusive rights of the coastal state to continental shelf resources have already been noted. So far as the outer continental margin (beyond the two hundred meter isobath) is concerned there are four possible types of arrangements which may in the future be adopted. One is to retain the present exploitability test, so that as coastal states acquire the ability to recover seabed resources at ever-increasing depths on the adjacent ocean floor their jurisdiction over the relevant area will correspondingly be extended seaward. Where the ultimate outer limit of such an advance would occur is still an unsettled issue.

A second arrangement would be for the coastal state's competence to be extended to a fixed limit on the ocean floor, regardless of the exploitability test. Various seaward boundaries have been proposed, such as the twenty-five hundred meter isobath, the point of contact between continental and oceanic type rocks (somewhere along the outer portions of the con-

---

[10] *Draft Ocean Space Treaty,* United Nations Doc. A/AC.138/53 (1970).

tinental rise), a fixed distance from shore—say one hundred nautical miles, or the outer edge of the rise itself. Still another alternative would be to set the outer limit of coastal state jurisdiction close to the coast, perhaps at the two hundred meter isobath; seaward of this point control over the resources of the seabed and subsoil would rest with an international authority.

Finally some sort of intermediate zone between the legally defined continental shelf and the deep ocean floor might be established, as in the US Seabed Proposal. The proposal is indefinite as to where the outer boundary of the Trusteeship Area would be; this point presumably is negotiable.[11] Beyond the Trusteeship Area is the ocean area where exploitation of seabed and subsoil resources would be under the control of the International Authority. It is not my intention here to go into the details of the US proposal, other than to note that I personally think the concept of an intermediate seabed zone is a good one, and to suggest that for both the landward and seaward limits of the Trusteeship Area some distance equivalency should also be included.

Turning now to the water column, it seems reasonable that some relationship should exist between a future juridical regime here and that applying to the ocean floor. There could, for example, be a zone of coastal state competence over the harvest of living resources out to the two hundred meter isobath—or fifty miles from shore if the distance equivalency were adopted. Within this zone guarantees could be worked out to protect the legitimate interests of foreign fishermen in coastal waters, and to ensure that those species not harvested by the nationals of the coastal state are made available for other fishermen to take.

Within the innermost fisheries zone the coastal state could have preferential rights to the fisheries, including fixed national quotas on preferred stocks, the power to license foreign fishermen, and the right to enact unilateral conservation measures. But even here, beyond territorial or other established limits, other countries would have the right to appeal what are seen

---

[11] See note 9 supra, Article 26.

as excessive coastal state restrictions to a tribunal established by the International Authority.

Seaward of this zone of coastal state competence would be waters under international control, as in the case of the ocean floor. The difference, if any, in regimes between the waters overlying the Trusteeship Area and those above the deep ocean floor might be, first, in the percentage of the revenues derived from the fisheries which would be allocated to the International Authority, and, second, in the amount of control the coastal state would have in the formulation and enforcement of fisheries management and conservation regulations.

There are, of course, many possible variations in a regime such as this; the important point is that some rational relationships be established between resource jurisdictions in the two environments, thereby responding to the legitimate concerns of the various groups within the international community.

Summary

The states of the world are facing a time of rapid change in the rules and arrangements relating to the control of ocean resources. The old regimes, based on the principle of maximizing the freedom of the seas, are fast disappearing, despite the best efforts of the developed maritime powers to arrest the trend. But opposing the drive toward expansion of coastal state jurisdiction to include virtually all the valuable resources of the world's offshore waters are the interests of many of the land-locked and shelf-locked states; these, together with the dozen or so major maritime powers which border on the open ocean, may be able to effect some sort of compromise between conflicting interests at the forthcoming Law of the Sea Conference. Only through the use of flexibility and skillful bargaining can there be any hope of viable and acceptable new regimes emerging from the Conference which will permit the continued and orderly development of ocean resources through the years ahead.

IV

A REGIME FOR WORLD OCEAN POLLUTION CONTROL[1]

E. W. SEABROOK HULL AND ALBERT W. KOERS

This chapter is concerned with the development of institutional, legal, and regulatory concepts for controlling marine pollution.[2] A fundamental assumption is that relevant and workable legal arrangements for such control are impossible unless they are soundly based on realities which are known and well understood by the designers of such arrangements. Such realities include environmental, societal, political, economic and financial facts and conditions as they exist in the world today and as they are likely to exist in the future. In the sense of the future are included the expectations of people everywhere.

Theorists and scholars occasionally base their thinking on facts and conditions as they believe they *should* be or as they *assume* them to be—the last derived, at worst, from hearsay or, at best, from the works of other scholars no better qualified than they to provide such bases in fact. Alternatively politicians and others with vested interests, though knowledgeable, may simply choose to ignore facts and conditions the admission of which would not serve their particular purposes. Unfortunately, these things seem to be more true for environment and ecology than for many older areas of interest. This chapter will present, in outline form, the factual bases on which any international

[1] The authors conducted the original research for this article while Fellows of the Woodrow Wilson International Center for Scholars.

[2] For the authors' views on a related topic, see E. W. S. Hull and A. W. Koers, *Introduction to a Convention on the International Environment Protection Agency*, Occasional Paper No. 12, Law of the Sea Institute, University of Rhode Island, September 1972.

regime for marine pollution control must be based—whether it be the regime offered herewith or another entirely different approach.

It is important to understand the meaning of key terms employed in this discussion. "Pollution" means simply the introduction to the environment as a result of human activities of materials and/or energy which alter its state and/or function and which may or may not obviously degrade its utility in respect of specific human activities and interests.[3] While admitting that major natural events[4] may pollute the environment by causing significant alterations of its state and/or utility, this paper is not concerned with such effects, since even theoretically major natural events are not subject to either legal or political control. By "environment" is meant basically the natural global environment. "Human activities" is defined generally but not exclusively as being of a technological and economic nature— i.e., of an *un*natural character. Finally, "marine pollution" means pollution of the ocean on a regional or global scale either on a short or long term basis.

The definition of pollution is not restricted by a requirement of evidence or proof of harm or damage as a result of that pollution. The reason is quite specific. The global ecology is a dynamic and finely balanced mechanism, the evolution of which has taken place through the whole of the planet's existence and through natural processes of infinite complexity and multiple and subtle interrelationships. It is difficult to conceive of a substantive alteration of the physical or chemical state of the ocean that would not have far-reaching repercussions—even though these may not be measurable or even identifiable at this point in time.

---

[3] Another definition views pollution as ". . . that part of the flow of materials and energy from man's activities to the environment that may cause undesirable effects," D. Serwer, *International Cooperation for Pollution Control*, UNITAR Research Reports No. 9, New York, 1972, p. 1 (reprinted in J. L. Hargrove, ed., *Law, Institutions and the Global Environment* (Dobbs Ferry: Oceania Publishing Co., 1972).

[4] The most commonly occurring major natural events which pollute the global environment are volcanic eruptions.

Present available knowledge of either the global or ocean environment is of such low order that we lack the competence to identify or predict with acceptable levels of confidence the consequences over the long term of virtually any change. Within present limitations of scientific knowledge it is quite possible for the conditions requisite to the onset of an irreversible reaction of catastrophic proportions to have been established entirely prior to first noticeable evidence of the initiation of such a reaction. One deals, in such cases, with rates and levels of introduction and accumulation ashore and in the atmosphere, rates of transport to and entrainment in ocean waters, lag times before a biological or other response sets in and achieves sufficient magnitude as to be evident, and the time, simply, before there is conscious scientific recognition that something is amiss. Thus, in the sense of global marine pollution, change as a result of human activities of such significance as to be measurable universally throughout all parts of the world ocean must be considered ipso facto to be unacceptable—at least until such time as the levels of knowledge and comprehension are sufficient to make safe and confident decisions to the contrary.

Clearly the definition of marine pollution as used here extends beyond merely dumping or accidentally discharging pollutants into the ocean from ships, aircraft or pipelines. As will be shown, marine pollution cannot be separated and isolated from global pollution generally. Indeed it is an avoidance of reality, which will assure failure of any such effort, to turn one's back on the land, to ignore the atmosphere and then to try to develop effective means for the international control of pollution of the marine environment alone. Ocean pollution cannot be controlled unless the release of the materials that pollute the ocean can be controlled. These are generated mainly by activities entirely within the boundaries of states and they are transported primarily by the atmosphere, secondarily by rivers and only tertiarily by specific acts of man. Thus, ocean pollution control requires the control of human polluting activities everywhere. It is as simple as that.

Finally, this work is primarily a theoretical approach in order to establish and clarify basic principles and concepts without confusing that effort by over-consideration of the details of implementation—some of which, admittedly, pose major problems in themselves. This approach is necessary since there has been and continues to be too great an emphasis on the treatment of symptoms and/or of the more notorious aspects of the problem while ignoring more serious causes.

Nature, Origins, Vectors and Fates of Global Marine Pollution

As a result primarily of man's technico-economic activities and secondarily of rising populations, increasing volumes of large numbers of materials—some natural, some alien to nature—are being released into the marine environment. Some are degraded naturally and removed from circulation and do not appear to be accumulating in or otherwise impacting on the natural environment. Some are known to be accumulating on a global basis; a rather larger number is on the suspect list. Some materials that do not show up as global pollutants nevertheless pose serious regional problems. Many of the indicted materials are not waste in the sense of trash, garbage, industrial waste or sewage, but are materials produced and used for productive purposes.

The effects of marine pollution vary widely and, at best, are known only imperfectly.[5] The effects of specific pollutants may be biological, chemical, physical, geological, or all of these.[6] They may be immediate and obvious—a toxic spill and massive fish kill, for example. Or, they may be subtle, not clearly identifiable or assignable—the weakening by chronic low level toxicity of one or more species with resultant long term alteration of the specific balance of the biomass; or the interference of an oily film with the sea surface exchange of gases and water vaporization. In the extreme, multiple and continuous poisoning

---

[5] National Academy of Sciences, *Marine Environmental Quality—Suggested Research Programs for Understanding Man's Effect on the Oceans* (Washington, D.C., 1971).

[6] *Man's Impact on the Global Environment—Assessment and Recommendations for Action* (Cambridge and London: MIT Press, 1970).

of the ocean could transform it into a biological desert. Were an oily film to become prevalent over major oceanic areas, not only would the carbon dioxide-oxygen balance of the air-sea system be materially intervened, but so also would evaporation of oceanic water with a concomitant reduction of rainfall ashore.

A more obvious effect of marine pollution is the reduction of man's marine food options, not only because of the destruction of particular marine species, but also because existing species may be made poisonous to man. Many pollution pathogens and toxicants are differentially concentrated by marine organisms—often to thousands of times ambient seawater concentrations. Such concentration is frequently cumulative through every trophic level of the marine food chain from microscopic phytoplankton through large pelagic predators (e.g., tuna and swordfish) which customarily grace our dinner tables.[7]

These are just a few examples of the adverse effects of marine pollution. More are known, and many more are probably unknown. Particularly unstudied and little known are the synergistic effects of one or more sublethal or subcritical pollutant levels which taken separately may be inconsequential but which taken together may prove devastating. The point to be made here is that marine pollution has ramifications which may be obscure to present science and a major threat to future human welfare: i.e., it should be, as it is, a major source of international concern.

In the sense of hard scientific fact, only a comparatively small number of materials have been identified as accumulating to a measurable degree in the global environment. By "measurable degree" is meant as indicated by time-series measurements over a number of years in disparate parts of the world. Among those indicated by such measurements are: carbon dioxide in the atmosphere, petroleum products mainly on the ocean surface, certain heavy metals and chlorinated hydrocarbons in the upper

[7] B. H. Ketchum, "Biological Implications of Global Marine Pollution," in S. F. Singer, ed., *Global Effects of Environmental Pollution* (New York: D. Reidel Co., 1970), pp. 190–194.

mixed layer [8] of the ocean, and artificial radionuclides in a larger and growing proportion of the oceanic volume. Although no other materials have been *positively* identified and measured as accumulating in the environment on a global scale, this does not mean there are not others. It means simply that we do not *know* of any. Lack of knowledge of a fact cannot be taken as evidence of its non-existence.

When emotion, false claims and suppositions are excluded, it is evident that we are dealing with a situation which is frightening not so much because of what we know but because of what we do not know at a time and place where change is rapid and the cycling times of most impacts are obscure. Where the knowledge does exist, every indication is that human activities are beginning to have a significant impact on the global environment—with particular emphasis on the ocean which in most cases serves as the ultimate sink for the effluents of civilization.

In the following brief summaries of individual classes of pollutants, the main objective is to demonstrate: (1) that emission sources are found almost entirely within the boundaries of sovereign states, rather than in international waters; (2) that such sources represent almost every facet of human technico-economic activity; and (3) that the primary vectors [9] for transporting these pollutants to the sea are natural (i.e., the atmosphere and rivers), rather than the result of human agency, and thus are not subject to effective control. These summaries are syntheses of a number of recent survey and original works[10]

---

[8] Generally speaking the ocean is strongly stratified with the lighter, warmer waters on top. There is very little vertical mixing except over very long periods of time. Mixing is largely limited to the upper one hundred or so meters (and, to a much lesser degree, the upper five hundred meters) ; here there is mixing because of the mechanical action of wind and waves.

[9] The term "vector" is used here in the sense of a carrier—e.g., the vector for a disease. It has the sense of carrying with direction, i.e., from source to sink.

[10] See notes 4 and 5 supra; see also FAO, *Report of the FAO Technical Conference on Marine Pollution and Its Effects on Living Resources and Fishing*, Rome, 9–18 December 1970, FAO Fisheries Report No. 99, Rome, 1971; National Academy of Sciences, *Marine Chemistry* (Washington, D.C.,

and represent the authors' best efforts to resolve apparent conflicts and discrepancies.

Heavy Metals

The National Academy of Sciences lists fourteen heavy metals currently produced by man and having a present or potential marine pollution impact. Of these lead has been measured as accumulating in the marine environment as a direct result of human activities. For mercury the indirect evidence is so strong as to force an assumption of fact, even though specific water measurement data do not exist.

Mercury—World mercury production exceeds 11,000 tons per year. Industrial and agricultural use releases 5,000 to 6,000 tons of this to the environment. Additional mercury is released incidental to other activities, such as burning fossil fuels (1,600 tons per year) and cement manufacture (100 tons per year). The natural flow of mercury to the environment includes two main sources: (1) degassing of the earth's crust placed, variously (depending on data base), at 25,000, 84,000 and 150,000 metric tons per year; and (2) the weathering of continental rocks, which is thought to account for the majority of the 3,800 tons per year estimated to be injected into the ocean by the world's rivers.

On the basis of these figures alone, human activity sources of environmental mercury would appear to be small and environmentally inconsequential. However, other data force us to reject this conclusion and, just incidentally, alert us to the danger of acting on insufficient knowledge. Ice cores taken from the Greenland ice cap show a 200 percent increase in the rate of atmospheric deposition of mercury over the last twenty-eight hundred years. A favored explanation for this phenomenon is that the rate of degassing of the earth's crust has increased

1971); J. P. Riley and R. Chester, *Introduction to Marine Chemistry* (London and New York, 1971); and S. Glasstone, ed., *Effects of Nuclear Weapons* (Washington, D.C., 1962).

proportionally and that this most likely results from man-caused alteration of large areas of the earth's surface—including deforestation, agricultural activities, construction, mining, etc.

Mercury International Control Criteria

(1)   Release occurs almost exclusively within the territories of sovereign states;

(2)   the primary vector is the atmosphere; and

(3)   the nature of the apparent major source (e.g., degassing) is such as to be virtually uncontrollable.

Lead—For lead, the Greenland ice chronicles show that, compared to 800 B.C., by 1750 there occurred a 25-fold increase in the annual atmospheric deposition rate; by 1940, a 175-fold increase; and by 1966, a 500-fold increase. The main cause to 1940 is given as smelting and since 1940, tetraethyl lead. World production of lead in 1969 totaled 3.5 million tons, of which some 1.05 million tons are thought to reach the marine environment; of this at least 350,000 tons are believed to be carried by the atmosphere. With an estimated input of lead to the ocean from the continental weathering process of 150,000 tons annually, the man-caused fraction stands out as the dominant factor. The majority of this input occurs in the northern hemisphere, reflecting the disparate levels of economic activity between north and south. And there, generally, it stays.[11] Between 1921 and 1966 a 350 to 700 percent increase in the lead concentration in the surface waters of the northern hemisphere was measured. The residence time of lead in seawater is several years; thus a reduction in lead pollution rates (e.g., ban on

---

[11] Because of the stratification of ocean waters (see note 8 above) and the nature of surface and near surface circulation of ocean waters, there is very little interchange of water masses between the northern and southern hemispheres except over very long periods of time, generally reckoned in centuries. To a somewhat lesser extent, the same is true of the circulation of the planetary atmosphere.

leaded fuels) might effect a substantial reduction in surface-water concentrations within a decade.

Lead International Control Criteria

(1)   Released entirely within national boundaries;
(2)   transported primarily by rivers, secondarily by the atmosphere; and
(3)   sources easily identifiable and susceptible of effective control without *undue* demand on either technology or economy.

Chlorinated Hydrocarbons

The most significant unnatural—i.e., not found in nature—materials being released to the environment are the persistent polychlorinated hydrocarbons, including: (1) agricultural and public health pesticides, including DDT, the aldrin-toxaphene group, and the benzene hexachlorides, (BHC) ; (2) the polychlorinated biphenyls (PCB) used in the manufacture of plastics, paint, rubber, refrigeration systems, and electrical and other components; and (3) others, including the dry-cleaning solvent perchlorethylene. All of these are highly persistent, i.e., they do not break down readily in nature. They are lipid-soluble and accumulate readily in fatty tissues of marine animals where they may produce a variety of adverse effects.

Data do not exist on the extent to which these materials may now be concentrated in *seawater,* but they are found in a wide variety of marine animals taken from widely scattered areas of both the open ocean and coastal waters. They are found in ice and snow taken from Greenland and Antarctica. Virtually without exception, marine birds, which feed almost exclusively on fish, are found to be contaminated with these materials.

Pesticides—Global production of DDT, aldrin-toxaphene and BHC is estimated at 100,000 tons per year each, of which at least 25,000 tons per year each of DDT and aldrin-toxaphene and 50,000 tons of BHC reach the sea apparently almost entirely via the atmosphere. Cumulative output to date is several million tons.

Polychlorinated biphenyls—Global production of PCB is estimated at 50,000 to 100,000 tons per year,[12] with total production to date probably of one million tons. About twenty-five percent each year leaks to the environment—eighty percent via the atmosphere, twenty percent via rivers. One set of data shows a general concentration in the open ocean biomass of one hundred parts per billion compared to one hundred parts per million in the freshwater and coastal biomass of Japan. Many PCB substitutes also are highly toxic.

Perchlorethylene—US consumption of perchlorethylene is running 360,000 tons per year, a quite substantial portion of which is believed to go into the ocean, primarily via the atmosphere.

If all production and use of these materials were to cease now, their concentration in the marine environment would continue to increase for some years as the continental load continued to migrate to the sea. One exercise in the use of global mathematical models and computers for analysis and prediction[13] shows that if global use of DDT were reduced to zero (straight line reduction) between 1970 and the year 2000, it would be 1981 before the levels found in fish peaked and 1995 before they again declined to 1970 levels.

Chlorinated Hydrocarbon International Control Criteria

(1) Released entirely within national territories;
(2) transported mainly by the atmosphere; and
(3) used for a wide variety of purposes, the control of which probably would be possible only by barring their original production.

---

[12] Production figures of individual manufacturers of PCB's and many other industrial chemicals are considered proprietary for competitive reasons, and since there are seldom any laws requiring their publication, generally speaking, they are not reported.

[13] D. H. Meadows, D. L. Meadows, J. Randers and W. W. Behrens III, *The Limits to Growth* (New York: Universe Books, 1972), p. 82.

Petroleum

Petroleum, since it is a natural product, is degraded in the environment, mainly by bacteria. The question is whether man-caused releases are exceeding that natural capacity for removal. Global production of crude oil totalled 1,820 million tons in 1969. Some 1,180 million tons of crude and refined products were transported by ocean tankers. By 1980 these figures are expected to be 4,000 million and 2,700 million tons, respectively. Using 1969 as the data year, the total yearly budget for *direct* and *indirect* contributions of petroleum products (as a result of human activities) to the marine environment shows a flux that may reach one hundred million tons per year, over ninety-five percent of which is airborne. Estimates place the total of petroleum products entering the environment as a direct effect of man's activities at 2.6 million tons per year, including (millions of tons) : offshore well seepage, 1.5; tanker operations, 0.5; other ship operations, 0.5; accidental spills, 0.2; dumping, 0.5; refinery operations, 0.35; and industrial and automotive wastes, 0.45. The indirect contribution is placed at 90 million tons or more, consisting mainly of vaporized petroleum products used ashore—gasoline, for example, during its various modes of transport, transfer, and storage. This fraction is transported entirely by the atmosphere.

In contrast, only about 100,000 tons per year are believed to be released to the sea as a result of natural seepage from submarine deposits. An additional unknown quantity of light petroleum derivatives (methane, ethane, etc.) is released to atmosphere as metabolites of some terrestrial plants and as natural decay products of organic matter.

Petroleum International Control Criteria

(1) Most releases occur within national territories;
(2) transported mainly by the atmosphere; and
(3) primary emission sources readily identified and defined, but widespread and vested nature of such sources may make effective control difficult.

Radionuclides

The natural background load of radioactivity in the world ocean is calculated at some 500,000 million curies, some ninety percent of which is caused by naturally occurring potassium-40. Through 1970, thirty years of nuclear weapons testing has produced an artificial radioactivity load of approximately 1,000 million curies—0.002 of the natural level. Most of this is still in the surface layer of the ocean; most is still in the northern hemisphere.

One estimate is that if nuclear testing continues through the year 2000 at its 1968–1970 average rate, the oceanic load from this source will be of the same order of magnitude as it is today. Projecting nuclear electric power capacity[14] through the year 2000 results in a radioactivity load from that source equal approximately to 0.0002 of the natural load. Statistically, these levels would seem to be insignificant. However, it is more complex than that. The concentration of nuclear power plants quite possibly will produce regional concentrations of radionuclides many times higher than the global average. Further, such radionuclides represent a variety of elements—some with long half-lives, some with a proclivity for concentration by the marine biomass. Strontium-90, for example, has a twenty-five year half-life and substitutes readily for calcium in the skeletal structures of biological systems. Finally, since man-made radionuclides are present mainly in the near surface waters, their concentrations are rather greater there than if they were uniformly diffused throughout the total oceanic watermass.

Radionuclide International Control Criteria

(1) Most activities occur within sovereign territories;
(2) where weapons testing is concerned, the atmosphere is the primary carrier, and where electric power generation is concerned, the rivers (and possibly dumping) are the main vectors; and

[14] The term "nuclear power capacity" as used here also includes the reprocessing of used nuclear fuel elements.

(3)   virtually all such activities are specifically identifiable and controllable.

Thermal Energy

The earth is basically a solar energy machine in perfect balance, that is, it reradiates back to space exactly the same amount of energy it receives from the sun. Were this balance intervened, as from a rise in carbon dioxide in the atmosphere,[15] the mean planetary temperature would change. In the case of the "greenhouse effect" it would rise. Substantial amounts of energy injected into the system from other, non-solar sources would also change the planet's thermal energy balance, with a concomitant rise in planetary temperatures.[16] Both fossil and nuclear fuels constitute such "other sources." The fossil fuels now being used with increasing rapidity went into storage (originally solar energy) only over very long periods of geological time. Since such energy is being released much more rapidly than it is currently going into storage, this constitutes a non-equilibrium energy source. Similarly, nuclear fuels went into storage at the geological "instant" of the Earth's formation; their energy release is clearly of a non-equilibrium nature since basically none is now going into storage.

Presently, the energy input to the Earth system from such

[15] Insolation (solar radiation received over a given area) consists of a greater proportion of short wave energy—to which carbon dioxide generally is transparent—whereas reradiation from the Earth surface consists of a greater proportion of long wave energy which tends to be absorbed by carbon dioxide, thus preventing its escape and holding it within the Earth energy system. This is the "greenhouse effect."

[16] The Stefan-Boltzmann Law is a quantification of the Stewart-Kirchoff Law which states, in effect, that a body in thermal equilibrium gives out just as much energy in radiation as it absorbs from the radiation that falls on it. The Stefan-Boltzmann Law states that the total energy of radiation R coming from a body is proportional to the fourth power of the absolute temperature, or where C is constant: $R = CT^4$. For a black body (which, for these purposes, the Earth approximates), $C = 1.30 \times 10^{-12}$ gram calories per second per square centimeter. Average insolation amounts to 4.6×10^{-3} gram calories per square centimeter per second. Using these figures it is not difficult to estimate the effects of various levels of input of non-equilibrium energy to the Earth system as a percentage of insolation.

sources amounts to only about 0.01 percent of insolation. However, the doubling time of energy use from such sources is estimated as low as twelve years and is diminishing. Within a century or so it could reach as much as five percent of insolation—enough to cause an increase in the mean Earth temperature of several degrees. This might be enough to melt the Polar ice caps, with a correlate rise in sealevel of some two hundred feet—enough to inundate much of the presently populated land area, including most of the presently highly developed regions. This seems remote until one considers the time and cost involved in the development of alternative and economic sources of energy (almost certainly solar) and the time necessary for the economic (i.e., gradual) replacement of a more conventional existing plant.

Thermal Energy International Control Criteria

(1) Released mainly within national territories;
(2) transported and stored by atmosphere, rivers and ocean; and
(3) readily quantified and identified but controllable only by the substitution of equilibrium for non-equilibrium sources.

Physical and Philosophical Bases of International Pollution Control

Physical Limits

Whether large or small, simple or complex, any discrete system has limits. Earth's planetary ecosystem is no exception. It has precise limits; only our knowledge is imprecise. The accelerated accumulation of certain pollutants in the global environment means those limits are being exceeded which, in turn, leads to the conclusion that man now has the capacity to impact materially and adversely on his environment. This fact is no longer in question. Still unanswered are such questions as:

Which pollutants in what quantities produce what kinds of perturbations? How much change is *safe* in respect of continued support of human life? How much change is *acceptable* in respect of the fulfillment of human and national expectations? Who is to decide? How is it to be controlled? Who pays?

Some questions are answerable only with additional knowledge of the functional dynamics of the planetary ecosystem. Others will be resolved only through the interplay of necessity, logic, economics and politics. There will be compromise, but this is permissible only in terms of politics and economics, for environmental compromise with absolute global limits would be no compromise at all. It would be a failure to control and quite probably a catastrophic one.

Since major pollutant accumulation rates correlate to their rates of release by man, it has to be assumed that human activities are directly and solely responsible. The causative activities, therefore, have to be controlled, and the level of control logically derives from a proration of the physical limits of the natural environment.

Inherent Right to Pollute

Were Earth ecosystem limits known absolutely and in detail, division of these limits by the number of present and potential polluters would yield an "individual right to pollute." The establishment of absolute—in the sense of basic life-support functions—physical limits is a matter for science. The definition and specification of an *acceptable* global environment is a matter of ethics and politics. Determination of the correlate release levels requisite to maintenance of the global environment within such acceptable descriptors, again, is a matter for science; it is a function purely of cause-and-effect relationships subject to neither political nor economic compromise.

Since neither absolute nor acceptable limits are known, initial reliance must be placed on *safe* limits. These are confidence limits based on a fine balancing of what is known with an awareness of how much remains unknown, to wit: "We are confident that if we remain within these limits it will be environmentally safe." It is a simple process to describe but far more difficult to implement. Not only do scientists and politicians alike disagree among themselves as to both fact and concept, but far more subtle points must yet be resolved. Though their resolution transcends the scope of this paper, in hopes of stimulating productive thought, some of the questions are asked herewith without in any way indicating answers: What precisely is involved in the concept of "inherent right to pollute"? By "individual," is reference solely to states, solely to persons, or to some as-yet-undeveloped "international (or environmental?) juridical individual" derived from an amalgamation of both?[17] Do old states have more right to pollute than new states? States with high population densities more right than states with low population densities? Under customary international law have polluter states established a legal right to pollute simply because they have been polluting for a long period of time without material complaint or effective contravention?

Polluter and Nonpolluter States

If planetary limits are being exceeded in the case of specific pollutants and if there are some states which clearly are emitters of such pollutants while there are other states which clearly are not significant emitters of such pollutants, it follows that some states must be exceeding their "inherent right to pollute" and that others probably fall far short of such limits. In this way, one can say that there are "polluter" and "non-polluter" states.

Available data show that level of economic activity is a close correlate of national pollution emission rates. Generally speaking, developed states are polluter states, while developing states are nonpolluter states. Since the pollutants of concern are a customary and proportional by-product of economic growth, it is clear that the imposition of global controls on the

---

[17] E. W. S. Hull, *The Earth Commons: Limits & Right of Access,* paper presented at the 138th Meeting of the American Association for the Advancement of Science, Philadelphia, 28 December 1971.

emission of such pollutants could seriously handicap economic growth in the developing states. Since the developed states enjoyed most of their economic growth with unrestricted, cost-free access to the environment (e.g., air and water) and since it is their continued polluting activities which might result in enforced inhibition on economic growth by developing states, it is almost certain that the developing states would not accept global pollution controls without appropriate compensatory provisions. Any international pollution control regime that is to be effective must resolve this problem in a manner that is both (1) fair and equitable to all concerned parties, and (2) acceptable environmentally.

Control Points

Whereas it may be argued and conceded that international dumping and accidental spills at sea beyond territorial limits contribute to the pollution of the marine environment, the available evidence shows that: (1) the overwhelming proportion of the offending materials are generated and released within national territories; and (2) the primary mode of transport from source to sea is not of human agency but, rather, of natural phenomena, i.e., the winds of the atmosphere and the waters of the rivers.

Since there is no conceivable way that winds can be stopped from blowing or that rivers can be prevented from flowing, it is a prima facie conclusion that the most significant modes of transport are uncontrollable. Thus, if control is to be effective, it must be exercised on the source. In no way does this abrogate the importance of regulating dumping at sea; it simply recognizes that such dumping is the lesser part of the problem, the control of which alone would not provide significant environmental protection.

Since states are sovereign and external interference in their internal affairs is unacceptable politically, states per se must be treated as emitting sources, and international regulatory arrangements devised accordingly. States are the logical control points from a world community point of view.

Control Mechanism

Logic suggests that if economic activity produces pollution, economics should be the key mechanism of control. Properly exercised, it is the most, if not the only, effective mechanism, for it treats with the root causes of pollution rather than merely with symptoms. A subconscious assumption of infinite environmental capacities and the nature of economic activity itself—along with, perhaps, distinctive relative value judgments—caused pollution to develop as a concomitant of economic growth. Even though its adverse effects now begin to be appreciated, it continues because, for the polluter, it is the least costly thing to do. At least, this is a widespread assumption.

Economic pressures are proposed (1) to take the profit out of pollution, and (2) ultimately to make the release of pollutants beyond acceptable levels an absolute economic liability. Not only would such pressures remove the economic incentive to pollute, but they would also serve to remove the fear of loss of competitive advantage by those who take specific and effective steps to reduce or entirely halt pollution. Whereas these economic pressures would be applied against states, the degree of that pressure should relate directly to the specific activities within states responsible for the emission of unacceptable levels of pollution transported beyond territorial limits.

An alternative might be to correlate economic pressures to environmental damage. This is considered to be impractical because (1) the valuation of such damage is too much subject to perspective variation and lacking of standard and universally acceptable criteria, and (2) because such valuations might or might not relate to economic incentives to pollute.

The following sections will attempt to show how the above premises might be employed in the design of an International Environment Protection Agency. They may demonstrate that it is possible for specific legal, institutional and regulatory arrangements to accurately reflect the realities of the global environmental problem as it presently, in fact, exists.

Basic Legal Principles of an International Environment Protection Agency[18]

Environmental Responsibility of States

A fundamental principle governing an International Environment Protection Agency must be that states be fully responsible for all activities subject to their authority which have adverse impacts on the quality of the international environment. This principle does not constitute a radical departure from existing practice.[19] It is, for example, an established role of *droit de voisinage* that a state is under an obligation to prevent use of its territory which is unduly injurious to the people of a neighboring state[20]—a rule most clearly stated in the decision of the Trail Smelter Arbitral Tribunal of 16 April 1938.[21] This case concerned damage to crops in the United States by fumes discharged from a smelter operation in Canada. The Tribunal held Canada responsible for this damage on the ground that "no State has

[18] For a discussion of international institutional needs in respect to the environment, see A. Chayes, "International Institutions for the Environment," in J. L. Hargrove, ed., *Law, Institutions and the Global Environment,* pp. 1–27; R. E. Stein, "The Potential of Regional Organizations in Managing Man's Environment," in ibid., pp. 253–293; George Kennan, "To Prevent a World Wasteland: a Proposal," 48 *Foreign Affairs* 401 (1968); R. R. Baxter, "International Cooperation to Curb Fluvial and Maritime Pollution," in *Proceedings of the Columbia University Conference on International and Interstate Regulation of Water Pollution,* 12–13 March 1970, p. 73; and U Thant, *Human Environment and World Order,* Address at the University of Texas, 14 March 1970, United Nations Press Release SG/SM/1259 (1970).

[19] For an analysis of existing arrangements and their potential, see L. F. E. Goldie, "Development of an International Environmental Law—An Appraisal," in J. L. Hargrove, ed., *Law, Institutions and the Global Environment,* pp. 104–165; and L. F. E. Goldie, "International Principles of Responsibility for Pollution," 9 *Columbia Journal of Transnational Law* 283 (1970).

[20] M. Sahovic and W. W. Bishop, "The Authority of the State: Its Range With Respect to Persons and Places," in M. Sorensen, ed., *Manual of Public International Law* (New York: St. Martin's Press, 1968), p. 316; J. Andrassy, "Les relations internationales de voisinage," 79 *Hague Recueil* 7 (1951).

[21] *American Journal of International Law,* 1938 Supplement, p. 163.

the right to use or permit the use of its territory in such a manner as to cause injury by fumes in or to the territory of another." Another area in which the environmental responsibility of states has found a certain degree of acceptance is in the international law of river basins.[22] An illustration is the recent Great Lakes Water Quality Agreement signed on 15 April 1972 by the United States and Canada,[23] whereby the two countries undertake to preserve and improve the quality of the waters of the Great Lakes and the St. Lawrence River. Another example is the 1963 Agreement in which the riparian states of the Rhine River established an International Commission for the Protection of the Rhine Against Pollution.[24]

The existing international environmental responsibility of states, however, has major deficiencies. This applies not only to its practical implementation, but also to its theoretical foundations. At the theoretical level, a first shortcoming is that enforcement is on a state-to-state basis only, rather than on the basis of individual state responsibility to the international community as a whole. The Trail Smelter case exemplifies this problem: Canada was held responsible because the United States decided to take action. If the fumes had caused damage outside the territory of any state—e.g., to the global environment generally—Canada most probably would not have been held accountable. Clearly, this deficiency in the environmental responsibility of states has direct implications for marine pollution: it implies that states are not responsible for pollution which reaches the waters of the high seas rather than the territory of a neighboring state.

A second shortcoming of existing environmental responsibility of states is that it is largely a responsibility for damages;

[22] See Stein, note 18 supra, pp. 265–274. For more general information, see L. A. Teclaff, *The River Basin in History and Law* (The Hague: Nijhoff, 1967); and A. H. Garretson *et. al.*, *The Law of International Drainage Basins* (Dobbs Ferry: Oceania Publishing Co., 1967).

[23] See R. B. Bilder, "Controlling Great Lakes Pollution: A Study in U.S.-Canadian Environmental Co-operation," in J. L. Hargrove, ed., *Law, Institutions and the Global Environment*, pp. 294–381.

[24] Discussed in Stein, note 18 supra, pp. 265–267.

states are responsible for the consequences of pollution rather than for its prevention. With the increased dangers and risks of pollution, and with the near impossibility of assessing damages from *global* pollution, prevention becomes an overriding consideration. One of the major functions of an International Environment Protection Agency, therefore, would be to expand the scope of the international environmental responsibility of states.

Internal Non-Interference

A second basic principle governing an International Environment Protection Agency would be that *from an international point of view* what states do within their national territory is strictly their own concern,[25] provided that whatever they do has no unacceptable *cumulative* consequences outside their territory. Obviously this principle, in a sense, is a mirror of the first principle: if states are internationally responsible for preventing pollution that originates within their territory and then causes damage in the territory of a neighboring state, they are a contrario not internationally responsible so long as the pollution remains within their own territory. In reality, however, the situation is not so precisely differentiated: many pollutants (e.g., fumes) reach the territory of a neighboring state in at least limited concentrations.[26] Further, whereas such concentrations may be of no substantial consequence on a state-to-state basis, the sum total of all such emissions from all states may have global environmental impacts that are internationally unacceptable.

[25] For a review of pertinent national legislation, see G. Moore, *The Control of Marine Pollution and the Protection of Living Resources of the Sea,* paper prepared for FAO Technical Conference on Marine Pollution and Its Effects on Living Resources and Fishing, FIR: MP/70/R-15, 23 October 1970, pp. 7–23. Information on national action is also available in the national reports prepared for the United Nations Conference on the Human Environment, summarized in Woodrow Wilson International Center for Scholars, *The Human Environment,* vol. II, *Summaries of National Reports,* Environment Series 201, Washington, D.C., March 1972.

[26] As has been pointed out in an earlier part of this essay.

Thus, the value of this principle is that it illustrates that the international environmental responsibility of states is not a matter of absolutes but, rather, a matter of degree: states are responsible for pollution originating within their territories if it may *contribute* to unacceptable external consequences. Conversely, within their own territories states have complete freedom to establish their own standards so long as these standards do not have unacceptable external repercussions. This principle already has found a certain degree of acceptance in the international community. The 1972 United States–Canada Great Lakes Water Quality Agreement, for example, provides for Common Water Quality Objectives which would limit the quantities of polluting agents discharged into the Great Lakes.[27] The North Sea states also have recognized the need to limit the inflow of pollutants to the North Sea, but as yet they have taken no further action.[28] A major responsibility of an International Environment Protection Agency would be to participate in the definition of the point at which pollution originating within national territories becomes unacceptable internationally.

National Action in International Waters

A final basic principle must be that states are held responsible for pollution produced outside the national territory of any state and which is the result of activities of their nationals or of activities subject to their jurisdiction. This principle is included in a number of existing arrangements,[29] of which international agreements dealing with oil pollution are, perhaps, the most

[27] See, e.g., Article II and Article III.

[28] Most of the cooperation among the North Sea states is concerned with oil pollution; but see International Council for the Exploration of the Sea, Cooperative Research Report, series A, No. 13, *Report of the ICES Working Group on Pollution of the North Sea*, Copenhagen, 1969.

[29] Article 24 of the 1958 Geneva Convention on the High Seas, for example, requires all states to take action for the prevention of pollution of the sea by oil or resulting from the exploration of the seabed and its subsoil, *United Nations Treaty Series* (Vol. 450), p. 96.

important examples. The London Convention of 1954 on the Prevention of Pollution of the Seas by Oil[30] prohibits vessels of a certain tonnage from discharging oil or oily mixtures into the sea.[31] Enforcement of this prohibition is the responsibility of the flag state of the vessel concerned, although other states make available to that state evidence of alleged infractions.[32] Thus, under this Convention a state is responsible for polluting activities occurring outside its territorial limits on the grounds that the activities in question are subject to its jurisdiction. A similar obligation is contained in the 1958 Geneva Convention on the Continental Shelf: Article 5 (para. 7) requires the coastal state to take appropriate action for the protection of the living resources of the sea against harmful agents.[33]

While the importance of such existing arrangements should not be underestimated, there is little doubt that an International Environment Protection Agency both could and should make an important contribution towards their further development. Underscoring this need is the rising volume and variety of mankind's use of areas not subject to the territorial jurisdiction of any state.[34] It would be a function of the International Environment Protection Agency to define the responsibilities of states over activities of their nationals on, in or under the waters of the high seas.

[30] *United Nations Treaty Series* (vol. 327), p. 3; the Convention was amended in 1962 and 1969; see D. M. O'Connell, "Reflections on Brussels: IMCO and the 1969 Pollution Conventions," 44 *Cornell Law Journal* 161 (1969); T. A. Mensah, "The IMCO Experience," in J. L. Hargrove, ed., *Law, Institutions and the Global Environment,* pp. 237–253.

[31] Article I.

[32] Article VI. Such arrangements are also part of international fisheries agreements; see A. W. Koers, *The Enforcement of Fisheries Agreements on the High Seas: A Comparative Analysis of International State Practice,* Law of the Sea Institute, University of Rhode Island, Occasional Paper No. 6, June 1970.

[33] *United Nations Treaty Series* (vol. 499), p. 311.

[34] See *Marine Pollution and Other Hazardous and Harmful Effects Which May Arise From the Exploration and Exploitation of the Sea-bed and Ocean Floor, and the Subsoil Thereof Beyond the Limits of National Jurisdiction: Report of the Secretary-General,* GAOR, twenty-first session, UN Doc. A/7924, New York, 1970.

International Air and International Water

If the preceding outlines the general principles under which an International Environment Protection Agency would operate, what specifically would the Agency be protecting? The answer is simply the quality of the international environment, which consists of two main components: (1) international air; and (2) international water. The Agency's basic task would be to preserve at acceptable levels the quality of international air and international water. International air is the *substance* of all gases of the atmosphere which envelops the earth; international water is the *substance* of all water circulating in the planetary hydrologic cycle. Note that the terms international air and international water refer neither to area nor space, but to substances. This is a fundamental departure from traditional concepts of international law.[35]

Water circulating in the planetary hydrologic cycle[36] and gases of the atmosphere are inherently international in character. All states use international air and international water, but such use is temporary in nature. After use by one state or its nationals, international air or international water inevitably moves to the territory of a neighboring state or to an area not subject to the jurisdiction of any state. It is then used by other states and their nationals. Except in a very minor and transient sense, the substances of international air and international water cannot be held and possessed by any state. States have a right of access and use, not of express ownership. Thus, international air and international water are at once a resource which must be protected against pollution and vehicles for transporting pollution. The waters of the high seas, which represent the bulk of international water, demonstrate this dual nature clearly. Ocean waters, it should be kept in mind, also serve a third function—that of the ultimate sink for the majority of the pollution that escapes beyond national territories.

[35] Hence, the proposed name of the Agency is International Environment Protection Agency, rather than International Environment*al* Protection Agency.

[36] The main component of which is the water of the oceans.

Four Control Situations

If the three first principles of the environmental responsibility of states are combined with the concepts of international air and international water, it is clear that states must be made responsible for pollution of international air and international water which originates within their territories and for pollution by their nationals or by activities subject to their jurisdiction in areas outside the national territory of any state. Thus, if the International Environment Protection Agency is to give substance to the environmental responsibility of states, it is faced essentially with four situations which require international action. These are: (1) pollution of international air which originates within a national territory but the effects of which are felt outside such territory; (2) pollution of international water which originates within national territory but the effects of which are felt outside such national territory; (3) pollution of international air which originates in an area not subject to the national jurisdiction of any state; and (4) pollution of international water which originates in an area not subject to the national jurisdiction of any state. The next question, then, is: What action could an International Environment Protection Agency undertake with respect to these four regulatory situations?

Functions and Powers of an International Environment Protection Agency

International Environmental Standards

The quality of international air and international water can be defined in terms of the concentration of polluting agents in such air or water. Examples of polluting agents have been discussed already. A prime responsibility of an International Environment Protection Agency would be to determine the maximum permissible levels[37] at which polluting agents may be

[37] For a discussion of such maximum levels of concentration, see Serwer, note 3 supra, pp. 5–18. On problems of standard setting, see P. Contini and

tolerated in international air or international water at the point where such air or water leaves the national territory or at the point where it is disposed of in areas not subject to the national jurisdiction of any state. The Agency might, for example, specify the maximum allowable concentration of mercury in the waters of a river at the point where such river enters the territory of another state or the area of the high seas; determine standards to govern the level of discharge of oil from vessels into the sea; establish maximum levels of concentration at which DDT may be permitted in the air at a point where it leaves the national territory of a state; and so forth.

Two tasks would follow the determination of such maximum safe levels of concentration and discharge. A first would be to identify environmental protection priorities and determine in each case whether global action or, initially at least, regional action were required.[38] In the case of polluting agents assigned global priorities, the Agency itself would seek to implement global standards for maximum safe levels of concentration and discharge. If on the other hand the impact of a polluting agent were determined to be limited to a specific region, the Agency could refrain from taking specific action, provided that the states of the region in question acted on their own to bring the situation under control.[39] In this respect, states of a specific region should be free—as in the case of a single state—to adopt their own standards so long as the effects of pollution originating within the region produced no unacceptable consequences outside the region. Obviously, this would not relieve the states

---

P. H. Sand, *Methods to Expedite Environment Protection: International Ecostandards,* paper presented at the Conference on Legal and Institutional Responses to Problems of the Global Environment, sponsored by the American Society of International Law and the Carnegie Endowment for International Peace, September 1971. For a survey of existing standards see Serwer, note 3 supra, pp. 51–58.

[38] For a discussion of the interaction between pollution control on a regional level and on a global level, see Z. J. Slouka, "International Environmental Controls in the Scientific Age," in J. L. Hargrove, ed., *Law, Institutions and the Global Environment,* pp. 222–232.

[39] Examples of such regions are the North Sea, the Baltic Sea and the Mediterranean Sea.

concerned of the responsibility to control levels at which their nationals or activities subject to their jurisdiction discharged polluting agents in areas not subject to the national jurisdiction of any state.

Control of Ocean Dumping

The foregoing tasks would not be adequate if specific arrangements were not made to cover dumping.[40] Dumping, in the sense used here, is the intentional discharge of large and usually concentrated amounts of polluting agents into international air and international water in areas not subject to the jurisdiction of any state.[41] Were states to collect polluting agents at the source and dump these agents in the waters of the high seas, this would circumvent any standards confined to setting maximum levels at which polluting agents could be permitted in international air or international water at a point where such air or water leaves the national territory. Even if states were to dump polluting agents in containerized form, standards might yet be circumvented, since there is no guarantee that the containers will remain intact. Therefore, the regulatory functions of an International Environment Protection Agency would have to extend to the control of *all* forms of dumping. The Agency might, for example, prohibit the dumping of certain polluting agents completely; make dumping subject to prior agency approval; and/or specify standards concerning the containers in which polluting agents could be disposed.

Action Alternatives

How might Agency standards concerning maximum levels of concentration and discharge be legally applied? Essentially, there

---

[40] A number of international agreements are being prepared for the purpose of controlling dumping; see e.g., *Draft Articles on Ocean Dumping Prepared for the United Nations Conference on the Human Environment,* XI *International Legal Materials* 19 (1972) ; in October 1971 an agreement was signed under which dumping in the northeast Atlantic would be prohibited, XI *International Legal Materials* 262 (1972) .

[41] See O. Schachter and D. Serwer, "Marine Pollution Problems and Remedies," 65 *American Journal of International Law* 105 (1971) .

are two alternatives:[42] (1) such standards might be made universally binding, and states simply prohibited from violating them; or (2) such standards might be used as the bases for a levy system. The first alternative would probably be unacceptable to states for political reasons. In practice rigid prohibitions of this nature have seldom proved effective. Further, it is an approach with a minimum of flexibility.[43] A levy system, on the other hand, would be more acceptable politically, and could be effective in adjusting the aforementioned economic specifics of pollution control to the needs of environmental control.[44] In this approach, a state would not be prohibited from exceeding a maximum safe level of concentration or discharge, but it would be required to pay a certain levy to the Agency. Flexibility and acceptability of this approach derive primarily from the fact that levies would correlate to a variety of factors and could be used for a number of purposes.

The Levy System

Levy rates might be determined, variously, by assessing (1) the economic value realized from polluting; (2) the degree to which states exceed maximum levels of concentration; (3) the period of time during which such excessive levels of concentration are permitted to continue; and (4) the per capita national product of states.[45] The first three factors relate to the fact that polluting offers a competitive advantage to states: control usually is costly and adversely affects the competitive position of states taking such control action vis-a-vis states which do not take such action.[46] Initially, such levies might be designed simply to remove this competitive advantage. With the passage

---

[42] Serwer, note 3 supra, pp. 18–25.

[43] In certain cases, however, this inflexibility may be precisely the reason for preferring complete prohibition: a certain form of pollution may involve such serious risks that only a complete prohibition is acceptable.

[44] Serwer, note 3 supra, p. 22.

[45] Ibid., pp. 22–25.

[46] General Agreement on Tariffs and Trade, *Industrial Pollution Control and International Trade*, GATT Studies in International Trade No. 1, July 1971.

of time without remedy, however, levy rates could be increased to levels where they constituted a distinct economic or competitive disadvantage. This is the principle of applying an economic cure to an economic ill. Levies would be assessed against states, and states responsible for similar levels of pollution escaping beyond their national territories would pay uniform levies.

However, as has been discussed, there would be a major exception to equity in the application of the above criteria for the assessment of levies. Developed states realized their initial economic growth under conditions of free, laissez-faire access to international air and international water. If the principle of maximum levels of permissible concentration were applied without modification to *all* states, developing states during their period of major economic growth would be deprived of such a cost advantage. In a sense their future economic growth would be penalized because of past economic growth of the developed states.[47] Equitable application and administration of the levy system could eliminate this apparent disparity in opportunities and sustain the expectations of developing states. Since, as has been shown,[48] there are polluter states and nonpolluter states and since pollution emission levels are directly proportional to some function of Gross National Product or Per Capita National Product, such an economic statistic may serve as a simple and feasible indicator of differential levy rates. Further, since it is hoped and expected that developing states will order their economic growth in such a manner as to minimize the pollution impact of this growth, the revenues to the Agency from levies might be used, in part at least, to offset the added cost of economic growth resulting from effective pollution control measures.[49] It should be emphasized that the proposal here is

[47] The United Nations Conference on the Human Environment (Stockholm, 1972) demonstrated clearly the resulting polarization between developed and developing countries.

[48] See pp. 98–99 supra.

[49] Technical assistance programs could assist in overcoming these problems, but they suffer in most cases from a lack of funds; see Serwer, note 3 supra, pp. 31–35.

not to use levy revenues to finance economic growth per se but only to finance the added expense of realizing such growth under conditions of environmental responsibility.

The functions to be performed under such a levy system by an International Environment Protection Agency might be as follows. First, the Agency would actively participate in its formulation, including the development of criteria on which the collection and redistribution of levies would be based. If these criteria are to reflect the interests of all states, rather than a particular group of states, it would be necessary to ensure that membership in the Agency is not only open to all states, but also that it consists of a majority of all states. Second, the Agency would directly administer such a levy system. Levies would be paid to the Agency, and the Agency make them available to other states according to the established criteria. If acceptable to the member states, the Agency could also use the levies for other purposes, including, for example, the funding of environmental research and monitoring, the establishment of an environmental disaster fund,[50] and the provision of compensation to states suffering damage from pollution originating outside their national territories and for which no other means of financial recovery exist.

Organization of an International Environment Protection Agency

General Conference

In general the organizational structure of an International Environment Protection Agency could be similar to existing international organizations, which ordinarily consist of a Gen-

---

[50] A beginning of such an environmental disaster fund can be found in the special fund established by tanker owners under the TOVALOP and CRISTAL arrangements, [VIII *International Legal Materials* 497 (1969) and X *International Legal Materials* 137 (1971)], and in the international compensation fund for oil pollution to be created by governments [IX *International Legal Materials* 66 (1970)].

eral Conference, an Executive Board and an international staff.[51] Nevertheless, in the interests of institutional effectiveness certain departures might be made from existing common practice. The General Conference, normally a plenary body holding central decision making authority, might be more assured of the acceptance of its decisions were they to be taken by majority vote based on a system of weighted voting.[52] No attempt is made here to specify the weighting criteria. However, to be both politically acceptable and environmentally effective, such a system must reflect a number of factors, including the following: (1) population of states, since (a) it is people who pollute and (b) it is people who are most affected by pollution; (2) national land area, since such area is a measure of the politically established share of the total earth capacity apportioned to each state; and (3) national level of economic activity, since (a) this is the primary determinant of per capita national pollution emission rates and (b) this is a direct indicator of the ability to pay for remedial measures. Clearly, if all of these factors are taken into consideration, the computations involved in the development of a system of weighted voting could become so complex as to be generally misunderstood and, therefore, politically unacceptable. The real challenge lies in the development of a system that is both conceptually simple and properly representative of the rights and expectations of individuals and states.

Executive Board

The Executive Board, in turn, might consist of international officials appointed by the General Conference and owing their duty to the Agency and not to the state of their nationality.[53]

[51] For detailed examples, consult M. Sorensen, "Institutionalized International Co-operation in Economic, Social and Cultural Fields," in M. Sorenson, ed., *Manual of Public International Law*, pp. 605–671; and D. W. Bowett, *The Law of International Institutions* (New York: Praeger, 1963).

[52] Weighted voting exists, for example, in the International Bank for Reconstruction and Development; it is related to the financial contributions of member states.

[53] This would be analogous to the Commission of the European Economic Community.

The Board could possibly follow a departmental system under which each member would be responsible for a specific area of international environmental problems and administration. Such a Board would be in a position to give attention to the interests of all nations, i.e., of the world community, rather than to the interests of specific states. The Board would not be the central decision making organ of the Agency, but it would carry on the business of the Agency in the intervals between meetings of the plenary group. It might be granted special powers, however, to exercise in the event the Conference could not reach agreement on specific measures, particularly where all member states had agreed that a problem was urgent in nature. For example, the Conference might agree that control of pollution by chlorinated hydrocarbons was indeed a matter of the highest priority but be unable to set maximum permissible levels of concentration. In such a case, the Board might be empowered to set provisional maximum levels based on the scientific recommendations of the Agency staff. These levels would be valid until rejected by a decision of the Conference. Such a procedure would be an additional guarantee that the Agency could indeed act effectively on an urgent environmental problem, regardless of political or other stalemates in the Conference.

Scientific Bases

Obviously, the decisions of the Agency would require a great deal of scientific information,[54] much of which might not initially exist. Two alternatives for obtaining such data would be available: (1) the Agency could adopt certain guidelines but leave actual investigations to the member states; or (2) the staff of the Agency and/or other more specialized UN agencies could carry out the necessary investigations on an international basis.[55]

[54] As pointed out in an earlier part of this essay.

[55] These two alternatives can also be found in the existing regional fisheries commissions; the Inter-American Tropical Tuna Commission, the International Pacific Halibut Commission and the International Pacific Salmon Fisheries Commission have an independent research staff, while the other commissions follow the first alternative. See FAO, *Report on Regulatory Fishery Bodies,* FAO Fisheries Circular No. 138, Rome, 1972.

There are advantages and disadvantages to both approaches. The positive aspects of the first alternative include lower financial needs of the Agency and a minimization of the political complexities that might arise where investigations were required within territories of member states on highly sensitive problems. On the other hand, internationally supervised investigations may provide a better guarantee of the impartiality of scientific findings, which in turn could have a positive effect on the acceptability of the resulting regulations. If the data were collected and evaluated by international rather than national experts, states could not advance the argument that such scientific findings merely reflected the parochial interests of specific states. The Agency might combine both approaches: i.e., leave data collection to the member states, with a relatively small international staff providing impartial validation and evaluation of such data. Such an approach would avoid duplication of the work of existing national and international organizations and would minimize Agency expenditures, while assuring that there is an available body of relatively impartial knowledge.

Summary

The foregoing discussion has outlined the nature of global marine pollution and the physical and philosophical bases for its control, and has provided a skeletal summary of one possible approach to the necessary institutional and procedural arrangements for international environmental control. The International Environment Protection Agency, as described, is largely a device for clarifying this approach. It is not suggested that the creation of such an Agency is a matter either of immediate necessity or even of ultimate desirability. Its functions could well be entrusted to existing international organizations or to more informal processes of decision making and action.

It is considered of crucial importance, however, that the world community take action to define the environmental responsibility of states. Participants in this process will range from states to individuals; its mechanisms will include international agreements, resolutions of international organizations, unilateral action and judicial decisions. To attempt to develop a scenario for this process would be a futile exercise. All that can be said is that it will be a process both of informal and formal growth, marked not only by agreement and success, but also by dispute, failure and frustration. It should be noted, however, that the time remaining within which action can safely be taken, like the environmental limits of the planet, is not infinite. The main purpose of this paper has been to suggest a conceptual framework which could serve as a reference in reviewing actual developments, and which, it is hoped, will of itself stimulate thought and discussion, contributing thereby to the international decisions and agreements which ultimately must evolve—hopefully sooner rather than later.

APPENDIX I

Schematic Representation
of the Seabeds and Ocean Floor *
(Showing the U.S. Proposal)

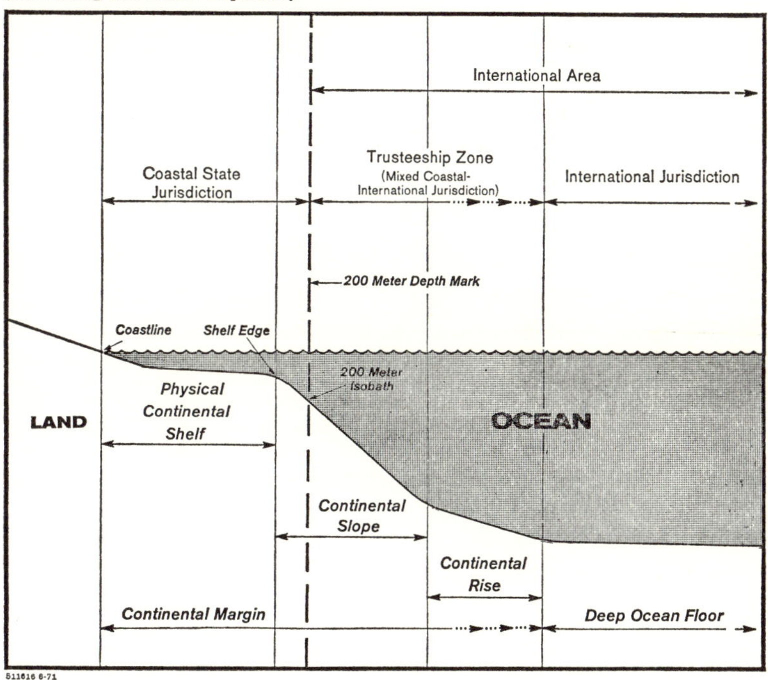

SOURCE: Office of the Assistant Legal Advisor for Ocean Affairs, Department of State, Washington, D.C.

APPENDIX II

CHART SHOWING NATIONAL CLAIMS TO JURISDICTION OVER THE TERRITORIAL SEA[a]

Extent of Claim (in nautical miles)	Number (and percent) of Claimants	Country (and date of claim)	
3	30 (25.6%)	Australia (1878)	New Zealand (1965)
		Bahrain	Nicaragua (1948)[b]
		Barbados	Oman
		Belgium (1929)	Philippines (1950)[c]
		China (Republic of) (1930)	Poland (1956)[d]
		Cuba (1936)	Qatar
		Denmark (1966)	Ras al Khaimah
		Fiji (1971)	Singapore (1878)
		Germany (East)	United Arab Emirates
		Germany (West) (1956)	Abu Dhabi
		Guyana (1878)	Ajman
		Ireland (1959)	Dubai
		Japan (1870)	Fujairah
		Jordan (1943)	Umm al Qaiwain
		Monaco (1967)	United Kingdom (1878)
		Nauru (1968)	United States (1953)
		Netherlands (1889)	Vietnam (South) (1965)
			Western Samoa
4	4 (3.4%)	Finland (1956)	Norway (1812)
		Iceland (1859)	Sweden (1779)
6	11 (9.4%)	Dominican Republic (1967)	Ivory Coast (1967)
		Greece (1936)	Malta (1971)
		Haiti	South Africa (1963)
		Israel (1956)	Spain (1957)
		Italy (1942)	Tunisia (1963)
			Turkey (1964)[e]
10	1 (0.8%)	Yugoslavia (1965)	

Extent of Claim (in nautical miles)	Number (and per-cent) of Claimants	Country (and date of claim)	
12	55 (47%)	Albania (1970) Algeria (1963) Bulgaria (1951) Burma (1968) Canada (1970) Cambodia (1969) Ceylon (1971) China (Peoples Republic of) (1958) Colombia (1970) Congo (Brazzaville) (1969) Costa Rica (1972) Cyprus (1964) Dahomey (1968) Egypt (1958) Equatorial Guinea (1970) Ethiopia (1953) France (1971) Ghana (1963) Guatemala (1940) Honduras (1965) India (1967) Indonesia (1957) Iran (1959) Iraq (1958) Jamaica (1971) Kenya (1969) Korea (North) Kuwait (1967)	Liberia (1967) Libya (1959) Madagascar (1963) Malaysia (1969) Mauritania (1967) Mauritius (1970) Mexico (1969) Morocco (1969) Pakistan (1966) Portugal (1966)[f] Romania (1951) Saudi Arabia (1958) Senegal (1968) Somalia (1967) Soviet Union (1960) Sudan (1970) Syria (1964) Tanzania (1967) Thailand (1966) Togo (1964) Trinidad and Tobago (1969) United Arab Emirates Sharjah (1970) Venezuela (1956) Vietnam (North) (1964) Yemen (Aden) (1970) Yemen (Sana) (1967) Zaire (1971)
18	1 (0.8%)	Cameroon (1967)	
30	2 (1.7%)	Gabon (1972)	Nigeria (1971)
50	1 (0.8%)	Gambia (1971)	
130	1 (0.8%)	Guinea (1964)	

Extent of Claim (in nautical miles)	Number (and percent) of Claimants	Country (and date of claim)	
200	9 (7.6%)	Argentina (1967) Brazil (1970) Chile (1953) Ecuador (1966) El Salvador (1950)	Panama (1967) Peru (1947) Sierra Leone (1971) Uruguay (1969)
20 to 200	1 (0.8%)	Korea (South) (1952)	
Less than 3 to 55	1 (0.8%)	Maldives (1968)	
Total:	117 (99.5%)		

[a] SOURCE: Bureau of Intelligence and Research, Department of State, "International Boundary Study—Series A—Limits in the Seas—National Claims to Maritime Jurisdictions," No. 36 (3 January 1972), revised 31 March 1972.

[b] No limit specified in 1950 Constitution.

[c] Modified in 1961 on basis of straight baselines.

[d] Partial jurisdiction claimed for additional three miles.

[e] Claims twelve miles in Black Sea as a matter of reciprocity.

[f] Claims contiguous zone to twelve nautical miles but silent on territorial sea.

APPENDIX III

SUMMARY OF THE DRAFT UNITED NATIONS CONVENTION ON THE INTERNATIONAL SEABED AREA*

On May 23, 1970, President Nixon announced a new oceans policy for the United States and stated that the United States would make specific proposals at the U.N. Seabeds Committee in August with regard to the proposed regime for the seabeds beyond national jurisdiction which he set forth in broad outline in his announcement. The submission of a Draft United Nations Convention on the International Seabed Area to the Seabeds Committee as a working paper for discussion within that committee, as well as with other governments and within the United States, implements the President's announcement. The draft convention and its appendices raise a number of questions with respect to which further detailed study is clearly necessary and do not necessarily represent the definitive views of the United States Government.

The basic structure of the convention reflects the President's proposals that states should by international agreement renounce their sovereign rights in the seabed under the high seas beyond a water depth of 200 meters; establish an international regime for the area beyond with certain basic principles and general rules applicable throughout this area; authorize coastal states as Trustees for the international community to carry out the major administrative role in licensing the exploration and exploitation of natural resources from the limit of coastal state national jurisdiction to the edge of the continental margin and to share in the international revenues from the Trusteeship Area which they administered; and establish international machinery to perform similar functions in the area beyond the continental margin.

Basic Principles

Among the basic principles which would become applicable to the entire International Seabed Area (including the International Trusteeship Area) under the convention would be the following:

* SOURCE: *Department of State Bulletin* 63:213–218 (24 August 1970).

121

The International Seabed Area would be the common heritage of mankind, and no state could exercise sovereignty or sovereign rights over this area or its resources or, except as provided in the convention, acquire any right or interest therein.

The International Seabed Area would be open to use by all states without discrimination, except as otherwise provided in the convention, and would be reserved exclusively for peaceful purposes.

Provision would be made for the collection of revenues from mineral production in the Area to be used for international community purposes including economic advancement of developing countries and for promotion of the safe, efficient, and economic exploitation of the mineral resources of the seabed.

Exploration and exploitation of the natural resources of the Area must not result in unjustified interference with other activities in the marine environment, and all activities in the Area must be conducted with adequate safeguards against pollution and for the protection of human life and the marine environment.

A contracting party would be responsible for insuring that those authorized by it (as Trustee in the Trusteeship Area) or sponsored by it (in the area beyond) complied with the convention. Contracting parties would also be responsible for any damage caused by those authorized or sponsored by them.

The general rules would be as follows:

Mineral Resources

All exploration and exploitation of the mineral deposits in the Area would be licensed by the appropriate Trustee in the Trusteeship Area and by the International Seabed Resource Authority in the area beyond, subject to general provisions relating to the terms of licenses included in appendices forming part of the convention, a number of which allow greater discretion to the Trustee State in the case of the Trusteeship Area. The contracting parties would have primary responsibility for inspecting activities licensed or sponsored by them. The International Seabed Resource Authority would also have authority to inspect and determine if a licensed operation violates the convention. Licenses would be revoked only for cause and in accordance with the convention. Expropriation of investments made, or unjustifiable interference with operations conducted pursuant to a license, would be prohibited.

Living Resources of the Seabed

All contracting parties would have the right to explore and exploit these resources (e.g., king crab) subject to necessary conservation measures and the right of the Trustee in the Trusteeship Area to decide whether and by whom such resources should be exploited.

Protection of the Marine Environment, Life, and Property

The International Seabed Resource Authority would be authorized to prescribe rules to protect against pollution of the marine environment and injury to persons and resources resulting from exploration and exploitation and to prevent unjustifiable interference with other activities in the marine environment.

Scientific Research

Each party would agree to encourage, and to obviate interference with, scientific research and to promote international cooperation in scientific research.

International Trusteeship Area

The provisions of the convention relating to the International Trusteeship Area would define the outer limit of this area as a line beyond the base of the continental slope where the downward inclination of the seabed reaches a specified gradient. Such gradient would be determined by technical experts, who would take into account, among other factors, ease of determination, the need to avoid dual administration of single resource deposits, and the avoidance of including excessively large areas in the Trusteeship Area. Other provisions would limit the Trustee's rights to those set forth in the convention. These rights of the Trustee State would include the issuing, suspending, and revoking of mineral exploration and exploitation licenses subject to the rules set forth in the convention and its appendices, full discretion to decide whether a license should be issued and to whom a license should be issued, exercise of criminal and civil jurisdiction over its licensees, and retention of a portion (a figure between 33⅓ percent and 50 percent is suggested for consideration) of the fees and payments required under the convention for activities in the Area. The Trustee State would also be able to collect and retain additional license and rental fees to defray its administrative expenses and to collect other additional payments, retaining the same portion as indicated above of such other additional payments.

International Seabed Resource Authority

The principal organs of the proposed International Seabed Resource Authority would be an Assembly of all contracting parties; a Council of 24 members, including the six most industrially advanced contracting states, at least 12 developing countries, and at least two land-locked or shelf-locked states; and a Tribunal of from five to nine judges elected by the Council.

The Assembly, which would meet at least once every 3 years, would elect members of the Council, approve budgets proposed by the Council, approve proposals of the Council for changes in allocation of net income within the limits prescribed in an appendix to the convention, and make recommendations.

The Council, which would make decisions only with the approval of a majority of both the six most industrially advanced contracting states and of the 18 other contracting states, would appoint the commissions provided for in the convention, submit to the Assembly budgets and proposals for changes in the allocation of net income within the limits prescribed in an appendix, and could issue emergency orders at the request of a contracting party to prevent serious harm to the marine environment.

The Tribunal would decide all disputes and advise on all questions relating to the interpretation and application of the convention. It would have compulsory jurisdiction in respect of any complaint brought by a contracting party against another contracting party for failure to fulfill its obligations under the convention, or whenever the Operations Commission, on its own initiative or at the request of any licensee, considered that a contracting party or licensee had failed to fulfill its obligations under the convention. If the Tribunal found the contracting party or licensee in default, such party or licensee would be obligated to take the measures required to implement the Tribunal's judgment. The Tribunal would have the power to impose fines of not more than $1,000 for each day of an offense as well as to award damages to the other party concerned. Where the Tribunal determined that a licensee had committed a gross and persistent violation of the provisions of the convention and within a reasonable time had not brought its operations into compliance, the Council could either revoke the license or request the Trustee Party to do so. Where a contracting party failed to perform the obligations incumbent on it under a judgment of the Tribunal, the Council, on application of the other party to the case, could decide upon measures to give effect to the judgment, including, when appropriate, temporary suspension of the rights of the defaulting party under the convention (the extent of such suspension to be related to the extent and seriousness of the violation). In addition, any contracting party, and any person directly affected, could bring before the Tribunal the question of the legality of any measure taken by the Council, or one of its commissions, on the ground of violation of the convention, lack of jurisdiction, infringement of important procedural rules, unreasonableness, or misuse of powers; and the Tribunal could declare such measure null and void.

The convention also provides for the establishment of three commissions, each of from five to nine members. The Rules and Recommended Practices Commission would consider and recommend to the Council adoption of annexes as described below. The Operations Commission would issue licenses for mineral exploration and exploitation in the area beyond the International Trusteeship Area and supervise the operations of licensees in cooperation with the Trustee or sponsoring party, but not itself engage in exploration or exploitation. The International Seabed Boundary Review Commission would review the delineation of boundaries submitted by the contracting parties for approval in accordance with the convention, negotiate differences among the parties and if the differences were not resolved initiate appropriate proceedings before the Tribunal, and render advice to contracting parties on boundary questions.

The members of the Rules and Recommended Practices Commission and the International Seabed Boundary Review Commission would not be full-time employees of the Authority.

The Secretariat of the Authority would consist of a Secretary General appointed by the Council and a staff appointed by the Secretary General under the general guidelines established by the Council.

Any amendment of the convention or the appendices would require the approval of the Council and a two-thirds vote of the Assembly and would come into force only when ratified by two-thirds of the contracting parties, including each of the six most industrially advanced contracting states.

Appendices, which are integral parts of the convention, are included in the draft convention by way of example only, as they require extensive consideration of the questions involved by technically qualified experts.

The illustrative appendices included in the draft convention relate to (a) terms and procedures applying to all licenses in the International Seabed Area; (b) terms and procedures applying to licenses in the International Seabed Area beyond the International Trusteeship Area; (c) terms and procedures for licenses in the International Trusteeship Area; (d) division of revenue; and (e) designation of members of the Council representing the six most industrially advanced states.

Appendix A, applicable to the entire International Seabed Area, would provide for non-exclusive *exploration* licenses not restricted as to area authorizing geophysical and geochemical measurements and bottom sampling and exclusive *exploitation* licenses including the right to undertake deep drilling which would expire at the end of 15 years if no commercial production were achieved. Deep drilling for purposes other than exploration or exploitation of seabed minerals would be authorized under a permit issued at no charge by the Authority, provided the proposed drilling would not pose an uncontrollable hazard to human safety and the environment. Appendix A also provides for certification by the Trustee or sponsoring party of the operator's technical and financial competence. Minimum and maximum limits on required license fees (the applicable fee to be specified in an annex to the convention with authorization to the Trustee or sponsoring party to impose additional fees within specified limits to help cover its administrative costs) are set out. Provision is also made for the categories of minerals and areas covered by licenses and relinquishment of part of the licensed area when production commences. Maximum and minimum required rental fees prior to and after attaining commercial production (the applicable fee to be specified in an annex to the convention) and minimum annual work requirements are provided for. Submission of work plans and data under exploitation licenses prior to commercial production and submission of production plans and reports are required. Rules are set forth with regard to unit operations. Appendix A further contains minimum and maximum required payments on production, the applicable amount to be specified in an annex to the convention (such payments to be percentages of the gross value at the site of oil and gas or minerals, to be proportional to production, and to be in the nature of payments ordinarily made to governments under similar conditions). The levels of payments on production and work requirements would be graduated to take account of probable risk and cost to the investor, including such factors as water depth, climate, volume, or production, vicinity to existing production, or other factors affecting the economic rent that can reasonably be anticipated from mineral production in a given area. Finally, the operator and the authorizing or sponsoring party, as appropriate, would be liable for damage to other users of the environment, and operators would be required to subscribe to an insurance plan or provide other means of guaranteeing responsibility.

Appendix B, applicable to the area beyond the International Trusteeship Area, would permit contracting parties to obtain exploration and exploitation licenses from the Authority if they designate a specific agency to act as operator on their behalf and to authorize persons they sponsor to apply for licenses. It would require the sponsoring party to certify as to the technical and financial competence of the operator and would require the Authority to grant licenses on proper application unless another application for the same block had been received at the monthly intervals at which applications were opened. If more than one application had been received, the license would be awarded in accordance with competitive bidding among the applicants. There would also be provision for award of a license by competitive bidding in the event of termination, forfeiture, or revocation of an exploitation license or sale of a block contiguous to a block on which production had begun or of a block from which hydrocarbons or other fluids were being drained. Appendix B would authorize transfer of an exploitation license with the approval of the sponsoring party and the Authority and the payment of a transfer fee. It would provide limits on the duration of exploitation licenses and would set out minimum and maximum work requirements, the applicable amount of such work requirements to be stipulated in an annex to the convention.

Appendix C, applicable solely to the International Trusteeship Area, would reaffirm the Trustee's exclusive right, in its discretion, to approve or disapprove applications for exploration and exploitation licenses and to use any system for this purpose. It would establish the term of the exploitation license and conditions, if any, under which it might be renewed, provided that continuance after the first 15 years is contingent upon achieving commercial production. Finally, appendix C would impose proration and set work requirements above the minimums specified in appendix A.

Appendix D would provide that the net income, after administrative expenses of the Authority, would be devoted to the economic advancement of developing states parties to the convention and would be divided among a list of stipulated international and regional development organizations, the list to indicate the percentages assigned to each organization.

Appendix E would stipulate the formula for determining the six most industrially advanced contracting parties for purposes of designation to the Council.

Annexes to the convention would be prepared by the Rules and Recommended Practices Commission, submitted for comments to the contracting parties and to the Council for adoption and would come into force unless more than one-third of the contracting parties disapproved within 3 months. In addition to fixing the level, basis, and accounting procedures for determining international fees and other forms of payment within the ranges specified in appendix A and establishing work requirements for the area beyond the Trusteeship Area within the ranges specified in appendix B, annexes could establish criteria for defining the technical and financial competence of applicants for licenses and would assure that all exploration and exploitation activities and deep drilling would be conducted with strict and adequate safeguards for the protection of human life and safety, the marine environment, and living marine organisms. Annexes would be drawn up to prevent or reduce to acceptable limits interference arising from exploration and exploitation activities with other uses and users of the marine environment, assure safe design and construction of fixed exploration and exploitation installations and equipment, and other related matters. Any contracting party believing that a provision of an annex could not be reasonably applied to it because of special circumstances might seek a waiver from the Operations Commission.

The convention would provide for due protection of the integrity of investments in the International Seabed Area made prior to the coming into force of the convention. Authorizations by a contracting party to exploit mineral resources of the International Seabed Area granted prior to July 1, 1970, would be continued without change after the coming into force of the convention, with the contracting parties being obligated to pay the production requirements provided under the convention. New activities under such authorizations would be subject to the regulatory requirements of the convention relating to pollution and unjustifiable interference with other uses of the marine environment. With respect to authorizations granted after July 1, 1970, the authorizing contracting party would be bound either to issue a new license in its capacity as Trustee or, in the area beyond, to sponsor the licensee's application for a new license from the International Seabed Resource Authority. A new license issued by a Trustee would include the same terms and conditions as the previous authorization, and the Trustee would be responsible for compliance with the increased obligations resulting from the application of the convention. Moreover, any contracting party authorizing activities after July 1, 1970, would be required to compensate the licensee for any investment losses resulting from the application of the convention.

DRAFT ARTICLES ON THE BREADTH OF THE TERRITORIAL SEA, STRAITS, AND FISHERIES SUBMITTED BY THE UNITED STATES*

ARTICLE I

1. Each State shall have the right, subject to the provisions of Article II, to establish the breadth of its territorial sea within limits of no more than 12 nautical miles, measured in accordance with the provisions of the 1958 Geneva Convention on the Territorial Sea and Contiguous Zone.

2. In instances where the breadth of the territorial sea of a State is less than 12 nautical miles, such State may establish a fisheries zone contiguous to its territorial sea provided, however, that the total breadth of the territorial sea and fisheries zone shall not exceed 12 nautical miles. Such State may exercise within such a zone the same rights in respect to fisheries as it has in its territorial sea.

ARTICLE II

1. In straits used for international navigation between one part of the high seas and another part of the high seas or the territorial sea of a foreign State, all ships and aircraft in transit shall enjoy the same freedom of navigation and overflight, for the purpose of transit through and over such straits, as they have on the high seas. Coastal States may designate corridors suitable for transit by all ships and aircraft through and over such straits. In the case of straits where particular channels of navigation are customarily employed by ships in transit, the corridors, so far as ships are concerned, shall include such channels.

2. The provisions of this Article shall not affect conventions or other international agreements already in force specifically relating to particular straits.

* SOURCE: United Nations Doc. A/AC.138/SC.II/L.4 (3 August 1971).

ARTICLE III

1. The fisheries and other living resources of the high seas shall be regulated by appropriate international (including regional) fisheries organizations established or to be established for this purpose in which the coastal State and any other State whose nationals or vessels exploit or desire to exploit a regulated species have an equal right to participate without discrimination. No State Party whose nationals or vessels exploit a regulated species may refuse to cooperate with such organizations. Regulations of such organizations pursuant to the principles set forth in paragraph 2 of this Article shall apply to all vessels fishing the regulated species regardless of their nationality.

2. In order to assure the conservation and equitable allocation of the fisheries and other living resources of the high seas, the following principles shall be applied by the organizations referred to in paragraph 1:

A. Conservation measures shall be adopted that do not discriminate in form or in fact against any fishermen. For this purpose, the allowable catch shall be determined, on the basis of the best evidence available, at a level which is designed to maintain the maximum sustainable yield or restore it as soon as practicable, taking into account relevant environmental and economic factors.

B. Scientific information, catch and effort statistics, and other relevant data shall be contributed and exchanged on a regular basis.

C. The percentage of the allowable catch of a stock in any area of the high seas adjacent to a coastal State that can be harvested by that State shall be allocated annually to it. The provisions of this sub-paragraph shall not apply to a highly migratory oceanic stock identified in Appendix A.[1]

D. The percentage of the allowable catch of an anadromous stock that can be harvested by the State in whose fresh waters it spawns shall be allocated annually to that State.

E. With respect to sub-paragraphs C and D above:

(1) [The percentage of the allowable catch of a stock traditionally taken by the fishermen of other States shall not be allocated to the coastal State. This provision does not apply to any new fishing or

---

[1] Appendix A is not attached.

expansion of existing fishing by other States that occurs after this Convention enters into force for the coastal State.][2]

(2) The allocation to the coastal State shall not be implemented in a manner that discriminates in form or in fact between the fishermen of other States.

(3) When more than one coastal State qualifies for an allocation of a percentage of a stock, the total amount which may be allocated shall be equitably divided in accordance with principles of this Article.

F. All States including the coastal State may fish on the high seas for that percentage of the allowable catch not allocated in accordance with this Article.

3. The provisions of paragraph 1 shall not apply in the event that States directly concerned, including the coastal State, are unable or deem it unnecessary to establish an international or regional organization in accordance with that paragraph for the time being. In that event:

A. In the case of a highly migratory oceanic stock identified in Appendix A, such stock shall be regulated pursuant to agreement or consultation among the States concerned with the conservation and harvesting of the stock.

B. In the case of any other stock, a coastal State may implement the principles of paragraph 2 provided:

(1) The coastal State has submitted to all affected States its proposal for the establishment pursuant to paragraph 1 of an international or regional fisheries organization applying the principles of paragraph 2;

(2) Negotiations with other States affected have failed to produce, within four months, agreement on measures to be taken either with respect to the establishment of an organization or with respect to the fisheries problems involved;

(3) The coastal State has submitted to all affected States the available data supporting its measures and the reasons for its actions.

The implementing regulations of the coastal State may apply in any area of the high seas adjacent to its coast or, with respect to an anadromous stock that spawns in its fresh waters, throughout its migratory range.

---

[2] It is the view of the United States Government that an appropriate text with respect to traditional fishing should be negotiated between coastal and distant water fishing states.

4. Enforcement of the fisheries regulations adopted pursuant to this Article shall be effected as follows:

A. Each State Party shall make it an offense for its nationals and vessels to violate the fishery regulations adopted pursuant to this Article.

B. Officials of the appropriate fisheries organization, or of any State so authorized by the organization, may enforce the fishery regulations adopted pursuant to this Article with respect to any vessel fishing a regulated stock. In the event an organization has not been established in accordance with this Article, properly authorized officials of the coastal State may so enforce these regulations. Actions under this sub-paragraph shall be limited to inspection and arrest of vessels and shall be taken in such a way as to minimize interference with fishing activities and other activities in the marine environment.

C. An arrested vessel shall be delivered promptly to the duly authorized officials of the State of nationality. Only the State of nationality of the offending vessel shall have jurisdiction to try any case or impose any penalties regarding the violation of fishery regulations adopted pursuant to this Article. Such State has the responsibility of notifying the enforcing organization or State within a period of six months of the disposition of the case.

5. The international or regional fisheries organizations referred to in this Article shall, *inter alia,* promote:

A. Cooperation with the United Nations, its specialized agencies and other international organizations concerned with the marine environment;

B. Scientific research regarding fisheries and other living resources of the high seas;

C. Development of coastal and distant water fishing industries in developing countries.

6. Exploitation of the living resources of the high seas shall be conducted with reasonable regard for other activities in the marine environment.

7. Any dispute which may arise between States under this Article shall, at the request of any of the parties, be submitted to a special commission of five members, unless the parties agree to seek a solution by another method of peaceful settlement, as provided for in Article 33 of the Charter of the United Nations. The commission shall proceed in accordance with the following provisions:

A. The members of the commission, one of whom shall be designated as chairman, shall be named by agreement between the States in dispute within two months of the request for settlement in accordance with the provisions of this Article. Failing agreement they shall, upon the request of any State Party, be named by the Secretary-General of the United Nations, within a further two month period, in consultation with the States in dispute and with the President of the International Court of Justice and the Director-General of the Food and Agriculture Organization of the United Nations, from amongst well-qualified persons being nationals of States not involved in the dispute and specializing in legal, administrative or scientific questions relating to fisheries, depending upon the nature of the dispute to be settled. Any vacancy arising after the original appointment shall be filled in the same manner as provided for the initial selection.

B. Any State Party to proceedings under these Articles shall have the right to name one of its nationals to sit with the special commission, with the right to participate fully in the proceedings on the same footing as a member of the commission but without the right to vote or to take part in the writing of the commission's decision.

C. The commission shall determine its own procedure, assuring each party to the proceedings a full opportunity to be heard and to present its case. It shall also determine how the costs and expenses shall be divided between the parties to the dispute, failing agreement by the parties on this matter.

D. The special commission may decide that pending its award, the measures in dispute shall not be applied.

E. The special commission shall render its decision, which shall be binding upon the parties, within a period of five months from the time it is appointed unless it decides, in case of necessity, to extend the time limit for a period not exceeding two months.

F. The special commission shall, in reaching its decisions, adhere to this Article and to any agreements between the disputing parties implementing this Article.

G. Decisions of the commission shall be by majority vote.

8. The provisions of this Article shall not affect conventions or other international agreements already in force specifically relating to particular fisheries.

APPENDIX V

TEXT

DECLARATION ON THE HUMAN ENVIRONMENT*

The United Nations Conference on the Human Environment having met at Stockholm from 5 to 16 June 1972, and having considered the need for a common outlook and for common principles to inspire and guide the peoples of the world in the preservation and enhancement of the human environment, proclaims:

1. Man is both creature and moulder of his environment which gives him physical sustenance and affords him the opportunity for intellectual, moral, social and spiritual growth. In the long and tortuous evolution of the human race on this planet a stage has been reached when through the rapid acceleration of science and technology, man has acquired the power to transform his environment in countless ways and on an unprecedented scale. Both aspects of man's environment, the natural and the man-made, are essential to his well-being and to the enjoyment of basic human rights—even the right to life itself.

2. The protection and improvement of the human environment is a major issue which affects the well-being of peoples and economic development throughout the world; it is the urgent desire of the peoples of the whole world and the duty of all governments.

3. Man has constantly to sum up experience and go on discovering, inventing, creating and advancing. In our time man's capability to transform his surroundings, if used wisely, can bring to all peoples

* Text provided courtesy of the Office of the Assistant Legal Advisor for Ocean Affairs, Department of State, Washington, D.C.

the benefits of development and the opportunity to enhance the quality of life. Wrongly or heedlessly applied, the same power can do incalculable harm to human beings and the human environment. We see around us growing evidence of man-made harm in many regions of the earth: dangerous levels of pollution in water, air, earth and living beings; major and undesirable disturbances to the ecological balance of the biosphere; destruction and depletion of irreplaceable resources; and gross deficiencies harmful to the physical, mental and social health of man, in the man-made environment; particularly in the living and working environment.

4. In the developing countries most of the environmental problems are caused by under-development. Millions continue to live far below the minimum levels required for a decent human existence, deprived of adequate food and clothing, shelter and education, health and sanitation. Therefore, the developing countries must direct their efforts to development, bearing in mind their priorities and the need to safeguard and improve the environment. For the same purpose, the industrialized countries should make efforts to reduce the gap between themselves and the developing countries. In the industrialized countries, environmental problems are generally related to industrialization and technological development.

5. The natural growth of population continuously presents problems on the preservation of the environment, and adequate policy measures should be adopted as appropriate to face these problems. Of all things in the world, people are the most precious. It is the people that propel social progress, create social wealth, develop science and technology and through their hard work, continuously transform the human environment. Along with social progress and the advance of production, science and technology the capability of man to improve the environment increases with each passing day.

6. A point has been reached in history when we must shape our actions throughout the world with a more prudent care for their environmental consequences. Through ignorance or indifference we can do massive and irreversible harm to the earthly environment on which our life and well being depend. Conversely, through fuller knowledge and wiser action, we can achieve for ourselves and our posterity a better life in an environment more in keeping with human needs and hopes. There are broad vistas for the enhancement of environmental quality and the creation of a good life. What is

needed is an enthusiastic but calm state of mind and intense but orderly work. For the purpose of attaining freedom in the world of nature, man must use knowledge to build in collaboration with nature a better environment. To defend and improve the human environment for present and future generations has become an imperative goal for mankind—a goal to be pursued together with, and in harmony with, the established and fundamental goals of peace and of worldwide economic and social development.

7. To achieve this environmental goal will demand the acceptance of responsibility by citizens and communities and by enterprises and institutions at every level, all sharing equitably in common efforts. Individuals in all walks of life as well as organizations in many fields, and their values and the sum of their actions will shape the world environment of the future. Local and national governments will bear the greatest burden for large scale environmental policy and action within their jurisdictions. International cooperation is also needed in order to raise resources to support the developing countries in carrying out their responsibilities in this field. A growing class of environmental problems, because they are regional or global in extent or because they affect the common international realm, will require extensive cooperation among nations and action by international organizations in the common interest. The conference calls upon the governments and peoples to exert common efforts for the preservation and improvement of the human environment, for the benefit of all the people and for their posterity.

Principles

States the common conviction that—

1. Man has the fundamental right to freedom, equality and adequate conditions of life, in an environment of a quality which permits a life of dignity and well being, and bears a solemn responsibility to protect and improve the environment for present and future generations. In this respect, policies promoting or perpetuating apartheid, racial segregation, discrimination, colonial and other forms of oppression and foreign domination stand condemned and must be eliminated.

2. The natural resources of the earth including the air, water, land, flora and fauna and especially representative samples of natural

ecosystems must be safeguarded for the benefit of present and future generations through careful planning or management as appropriate.

3. The capacity of the earth to produce vital renewable resources must be maintained and wherever practicable restored or improved.

4. Man has a special responsibility to safeguard and wisely manage the heritage of wildlife and its habitat which are now gravely imperilled by a combination of adverse factors. Nature conservation including wildlife must therefore receive importance in planning for economic development.

5. The non-renewable resources of the earth must be employed in such a way as to guard against the danger of their future exhaustion and to ensure that benefits from such employment are shared by all mankind.

6. The discharge of toxic substances or of other substances and the release of heat, in such quantities or concentrations as to exceed the capacity of the environment to render them harmless, must be halted in order to ensure that serious or irreversible damage is not inflicted upon ecosystems. The just struggle of the peoples of all countries against pollution should be supported.

7. States shall take all possible steps to prevent pollution of the seas by substances that are liable to create hazards to human health, to harm living resources and marine life, to damage amenities or to interfere with other legitimate uses of the sea.

8. Economic and social development is essential for ensuring a favorable living and working environment for man and for conditions on earth that are necessary for the improvement of the quality of life.

9. Environmental deficiencies generated by the conditions of underdevelopment and natural disasters pose grave problems and can best be remedied by accelerated development through the transfer of substantial quantities of financial and technological assistance as a supplement to the domestic effort of the developing countries and such timely assistance as may be required.

10. For the developing countries, stability of prices and adequate earnings for primary commodities and raw material are essential to

environmental management since economic factors as well as economic processes must be taken into account.

11. The environmental policies of all states should enhance and not adversely affect the present or future development potential of developing countries, nor should they hamper the attainment of better living conditions for all, and appropriate steps should be taken by states and international organizations with a view to reaching agreement on meeting the possible national and international economic consequences resulting from the application of environmental measures.

12. Resources should be made available to preserve and improve the environment, taking into account the circumstances and particular requirements of developing countries and any costs which may emanate from their incorporating environmental safeguards into their development planning and the need for making available to them, upon their request, additional international technical and financial assistance for this purpose.

13. In order to achieve a more rational management of resources and thus to improve the environment, states should adopt an integrated and coordinated approach to their development planning so as to ensure that development is compatible with the need to protect and improve the human environment for the benefit of their population.

14. Rational planning constitutes an essential tool for reconciling any conflict between the needs of development and the need to protect and improve the environment.

15. Planning must be applied to human settlements and urbanization with a view to avoiding adverse effect on the environment and obtaining maximum social, economic and environmental benefits for all. In this respect projects which are designed for colonialist and racist domination must be abandoned.

16. Demographic policies which are without prejudice to basic human rights and which are deemed appropriate by governments concerned, should be applied in those regions where the rate of population growth or excessive population concentrations are likely to have adverse effects on the environment or development, or where

low population density may prevent improvement of the human environment and impede development.

17. Appropriate national institutions must be entrusted with the task of planning, managing or controlling the environmental resources of states with the view to enhancing environmental quality.

18. Science and technology, as part of their contribution to economic and social development, must be applied to the identification, avoidance and control of environmental risks and the solution of environmental problems and for the common good of mankind.

19. Education in environmental matters, for the younger generation as well as adults, giving due consideration for the underprivileged, is essential in order to broaden the basis for an enlightened opinion and responsible conduct by individuals, enterprises and communities in protecting and improving the environment in its full human dimension. It is also essential that mass media of communications avoid contributing to the deterioration of the environment, but, on the contrary, disseminate information of an educational nature on the need to protect and improve the environment in order to educate man to develop in every respect.

20. Scientific research and development in the context of environmental problems, both national and multinational, must be promoted in all countries, especially the developing countries. In this connection, the free flow of up to date scientific information and experience must be supported and assisted to facilitate the solution of environmental problems; environmental technologies should be made available to developing countries on terms which would encourage their wide dissemination without constituting an economic burden on the developing countries.

21. States have, in accordance with the Charter of the United Nations and the principles of international law, the sovereign right to exploit their own resources pursuant to their own environmental policies, and the responsibility to ensure that activities within their jurisdiction or control do not cause damage to the environment of other states or of areas beyond the limits of national jurisdiction.

22. States shall cooperate to develop further the international law regarding liability and compensation for the victims of pollution

and other environmental damage caused by activities within the jurisdiction or control of such states to areas beyond their jurisdiction.

23. Without prejudice to such general principles as may be agreed upon by the international community, or to the criteria and minimum levels which will have to be determined nationally, it will be essential in all cases to consider the systems of values prevailing in each country, and the extent of the applicability of standards which are valid for the most advanced countries but which may be inappropriate and of unwarranted social cost for the developing countries.

24. International matters concerning the protection and improvement of the environment should be handled in a cooperative spirit by all countries, big or small, on an equal footing. Cooperation through multilateral or bilateral arrangements or other appropriate means is essential to prevent, eliminate or reduce and effectively control adverse environmental effects resulting from activities conducted in all spheres, in such a way that due account is taken of the sovereignty and interests of all states.

25. States shall ensure that international organizations play a coordinated, efficient and dynamic role for the protection and improvement of the environment.

26. Man and his environment must be spared the effects of nuclear weapons and all other means of mass destruction. States must strive to reach prompt agreement, in the relevant international organs, on the elimination and complete destruction of such weapons.

INDEX

Advisory Committee on the Law of the Sea (ACLOS): formation of, 16; functions of, 16–18; and special domestic interests, 16–19, 43; Fisheries Subcommittee of, 32–33; Marine Science Subcommittee of, 36; Hard Minerals Subcommittee of, 37; Environmental Subcommittee of, 42; International Law and Relations Subcommittee of, 42

Antisubmarine Warfare Tracking and Detection Devices (ASW), 24 passim

Arctic Waters Pollution Prevention Act of 1970 (Canada), 39 n, 40

Brittin, Burdick, H., 16 n

Chlorinated hydrocarbons, 87, 91–92. *See also* Pollution

Christy, Dr. Francis T., Jr., and criticism of US oceans policy, 15–16, 19

Commission of the European Economic Community, 113 n

Convention on the Continental Shelf (1958), 25–26, 35 n, 105

Convention on the High Seas (1958), 104 n

Convention on the Territorial Sea and the Contiguous Zone (Territorial Sea Convention) (1958), 23

Council on Environmental Quality, 42

"Creeping jurisdiction" argument, and the Department of Defense, 29

"Declaration and Treaty Concerning the Reservation . . . for Peaceful Purposes of the Sea-Bed and of the Ocean Floor . . . " (1967), 10

Declaration on the Human Environment (1972), text of, 135–41

Department of Defense (DOD), *see* Military

de Soto, Alvaro, 56 n

Distance equivalency concept, 75–76, 81

"Draft Articles on the Breadth of the Territorial Sea, Straits, and Fisheries Submitted by the United States" (1971), 12 passim; text of, 130–34

Draft United Nations Convention on the International Seabed Area (Draft Convention) (1970), 16 passim; jurisdictional zones described by, 26 n, 117 (chart); summary of, 121–29

Effective advocacy, 20–21; and marine science community, 35

Environmental disaster fund, 112

Environmental protection: as special domestic interest, 21, 40–43; US policy on, 41–42; area-specific nature of, 58–59; and the principle of "additionality," 60. *See also* International Environment Protection Agency; Ocean dumping; Pollution

Environmental Protection Agency, 42

Environmental responsibility of states, 101–3

Exclusive Fisheries Zone Act (1966), 30

Executive Branch, *see* United States Government

Fisheries: and ACLOS, 17, 32–33; as special domestic interest, 21, 30–33; and types of fishing fleets, 30, 69; and US-Brazilian treaty (1972), 31 n; US policy on, 31–33, 131–34;

143

global statistics on, 68–70; and types of fish, 68–71; jurisdictional claims to, 72; and extra-territorial zone, 78–79; and proposed juridical regime, 79–82. *See also* Ocean resources

"Free transit" through straits, 52

Goldberg, Arthur J., 11
Great Lakes Water Quality Agreement (1972), 102, 104
"Greenhouse effect," 95
Group of 77, and Seabed Committee, 45

Hard minerals: and "Deep Seabed Hard Mineral Resources Act" (1972), 13; and ACLOS, 17; as special domestic interest, 20–21, 36–38; and OCSLA, 36; and Draft Convention, 37–38; and US Congress, 37–38; types of, 71–72; and jurisdictional claims to, 72; and proposed juridical regime, 79–82. *See also* Ocean resources
Heavy metals, 87, 89–91. *See also* Pollution

"Innocent passage," 52
Insolation, 95 n, 96
Intelligence operations and traditional naval maneuvers, 23–24
Intergovernmental Maritime Consultative Organization (IMCO), 42; Conference of, 44
Intergovernmental Meeting on Ocean Dumping (1972), 40 n
International air/water, definitions of, 106
International Bank for Reconstruction and Development, 113 n
International Environment Protection Agency: proposal of, 100; legal principles of, 101–7; functions and powers of, 107–12; and control of ocean dumping, 109; levy system of, 110–12; organization of, 112–15. *See also* Pollution
International Law Commission, 52

International Seabed Area, 35; Draft Convention on, 121–29
International Seabed Resource Authority, 26, 41; in Draft Convention, 122
International Trusteeship Area, 26 passim; definition of, 29; and Draft Convention, 28–29, 121

Johnson, Lyndon B., 11

Law of the sea: proposed Third UN Conference on, 11, 44, 47, 55–56, 61–62, 65, 73, 82; and existing jurisdictional claims, 22 n, 59, 72–73, 118–20; and Seabed Committee, 44–46, 50–51, 53, 61–62; developed and developing countries' controversy over, 45 passim, 73–79; politics of, 46–53; 1958 and 1960 UN Conferences on, 47; and General Assembly, 47, 54–62; impending changes in, 73–79. *See also* Ocean regimes; United Nations General Assembly
Lead. *See* Heavy metals
League of Nations Codification Conference (1930), 46
Logue, John J., and ocean revenues, 51
London Convention on the Prevention of Pollution of the Seas by Oil (1954), 105

McKernan, Donald L., 32
Maritime transportation: US policy on, 13, 39; and ACLOS, 17; as special domestic interest, 20–21, 38–39
Mercury. *See* Heavy metals
Military: and ACLOS, 18; and problem of secrecy, 18, 20–21; as special domestic interest, 19–27 passim; and Polaris/Poseidon nuclear strike force, 22–23; intelligence operations and traditional naval maneuvers of, 23–24; antisubmarine warfare tracking and detection devices of, 24–26; and US ocean

proposals, 24–27 passim; "creeping
jurisdiction" argument of, 29
Mojsov, Lazar, 56 n

National Academy of Sciences, 36
National Petroleum Council, 27. *See
also* Petroleum and natural gas
National Security Council, 18

Ocean dumping, 40–42, 85, 93, 99,
105; definition of, 109; control of,
109–10. *See also* Environmental
protection; International Environment Protection Agency; Pollution
Oceanographer (research ship) , 11
Ocean regimes: US proposals on,
12–13 passim, 77, 81–82, 121–34;
jurisdictional types of, 67–68; and
existing international law, 72–73;
impending changes in, 73–75; and
the UN, 75; jurisdictional scope of
international authority in, 75–79;
and distance equivalency concept,
75–76, 81; and fisheries zones, 77–
79; and "patrimonial sea," 79;
principal interest groups involved
in, 79–80; Arvid Pardo's statement
on, 80. *See also* International
Trusteeship Area
Ocean resources: types of, 67–72;
management of, 75, 79–82; revenues from, 76–79; and exploitability test, 80. *See also* Fisheries;
Hard minerals; Petroleum and
natural gas
Ocean space, components of, 12 n
Operational code, and UN General
Assembly, 54
Outer Continental Shelf Lands Act
(OCSLA) , 36

Pacem in Maribus II Convocation
(1971) , 41
Pardo, Arvid, 10, 50, 80
Petroleum and natural gas: and
ACLOS, 17; and effective advocacy, 20; as special domestic interest, 21, 27–30 passim; and National Petroleum Council, 27; and
the "energy crisis," 28; US policy

on, 28–30; production estimates of,
71, 93; and maritime pollution,
87, 93. *See also* Ocean resources
Piccard, Jacques, 41
Pollutants, marine, classes of, 87–96
Pollution, definition of, 84
Pollution, marine: control of, 40–43,
85, 96–100; definition of, 84; and
global ecology, 84; and ocean
dumping, 85; effects of, 86–87;
sources of, 87–96; vectors of, 88
passim; safe limits of, 96–97; and
"inherent right to pollute," 97–98;
and national emission rates, 98;
and polluter and nonpolluter
states, 98–99; relation to economic
growth of, 99–100; and International Environment Protection
Agency, 101
Pye, Lucian W., 47 n

Radionuclides, 88, 94–95. *See also*
Pollution

Scientific research: and ACLOS, 17;
and effective advocacy, 21; as special domestic interest, 21, 33–36;
antipathy of developing countries
toward, 33–34; US policy on,
34–36; and environmental protection, 114–15
Seabed Committee. *See* United Nations Committee on the Peaceful
Uses of the Sea-Bed and the Ocean
Floor Beyond the Limits of National Jurisdiction
Solomon, P. V. J., 53
Special domestic interests: definition
of, 12; and administrative aspects
of foreign policy determination,
13–21, 43; criticism of US policy
by, 15–16; and ACLOS, 16–19, 43;
and government secrecy, 19; DOD's
inclusion among, 19–20; and effective advocacy, 20–21; categories
of, 21; response of US policy to,
21–43; and the national interest,
43. *See also* Environmental protection; Fisheries; Hard minerals;
Maritime transportation; Military;

Petroleum and natural gas; Scientific research

Stefan-Boltzmann Law, and thermal energy, 95 n

Stevenson, John R., 15 n, 26

Stockholm Conference. *See* United Nations Conference on the Human Environment

Strategic Arms Limitation Agreement (1972), and ASW tracking and detection devices, 27 n

Task Force. *See* United States Government Inter-Agency Law of the Sea Task Force

Territorial Sea Convention. *See* Convention on the Territorial Sea and the Contiguous Zone

Thermal energy, 95–96. *See also* Pollution

Third United Nations Conference on the Law of the Sea (proposed). *See* Law of the sea

Trail Smelter Arbitral Tribunal (1938), 101

Transnationalism, 65 n

Trusteeship Area. *See* International Trusteeship Area

United Nations Committee on the Peaceful Uses of the Sea-Bed and the Ocean Floor Beyond the Limits of National Jurisdiction: creation of, 11; and US draft treaty articles, 12; and ACLOS, 17; progress of, 44–46, 61–62; and problem of expertise, 53; complexity of issues facing, 61–62

United Nations Conference on the Human Environment (UNCHE) (1972), 42, 44, 46, 60, 11 n; Declaration of, 135–41

United Nations Conference on Trade, Aid, and Development (UNCTAD), 61

United Nations development fund, 50

United Nations Food and Agricultural Organization, 70

United Nations General Assembly, 10; politics of, 46–62; and controversy between developed and developing countries, 48–53 passim; and the problem of majoritarianism, 49, 52; negotiating style of, 52–53; and parliamentary diplomacy, 54; and "plurality of regimes," 55; as international lawmaking forum, 58. *See also* Law of the sea; Ocean regimes

United States Government: Executive Branch of, 13–14; Department of State, 14–16; and Task Force delegation, 15 n; Department of Defense, 18–27 passim; Department of Commerce, 19; Department of Interior, 19

United States Government Inter-Agency Law of the Sea Task Force, 15–18

United States oceans policy: definition of, 12–13; on ocean regimes, 12–13, 77, 81–82, 121–34; administrative aspects of, 13–21; on hard minerals, 13, 36–38; on maritime transportation, 13, 39; criticism of, 15–16, 18 n; and ACLOS, 16–21; substantive aspects of, 21–43; and military interests, 24–27 passim; on International Trusteeship Area, 28–29; on petroleum and natural gas, 28–30; on fisheries, 31–33, 131–34; role of Congress in, 37–38 n; on environmental protection, 41–42

U Thant, 10

Zero-sum game, 51